止 园 图 册

绘画中的桃花源

刘珊珊 黄 晓 著

中 原 英译

东华大学出版社
DONGHUA UNIVERSITY PRESS

The Zhi Garden Album:
A Portrait of
Peach Blossom Spring

Liu Shanshan and Huang Xiao

Translated by
Zhong Yuan

The Zhi Garden Album:
A Portrait of
Peach Blossom Spring

Contents

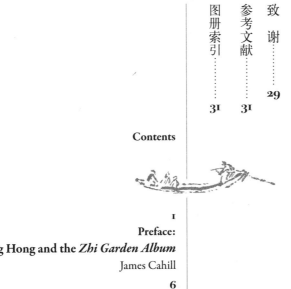

代序……张宏与《止园图》 高居翰

Preface:
Zhang Hong and the *Zhi Garden Album*

James Cahill

张宏是晚明苏州数十年来罕见的出色画家。

张宏，字君度，号鹤涧，生于 1577 年，约卒于 1652 年或稍晚。明代徐鸣时《横溪录》记载了张宏的生平。他居住在苏州西南十三里（6.5 千米）的横溪镇（今苏州市虎丘区横塘街道，Fig.1-1），少年时代读过书，也曾有求取功名的打算，但仕途并不顺利，后来迫于生计转向了绘画。张宏的作品充满古意却不拘泥于古，获得了很高的声誉。张宏的家庭异常贫困，一家老小以及贫苦的亲戚都仰仗他的一支画笔讨生活。但只要稍有宽裕，他就很珍惜自己的作品，不肯随便卖人。这则记载为我们勾勒出一位

Fig. 1-1
张宏故乡苏州横溪镇位置图
Location of Zhang Hong's hometown Hengxi

Zhang Hong was *the* outstanding painter of the late Ming dynasty in Suzhou for several decades.

Zhang Hong took the courtesy name Jundu, and also went by his nom de plume Hejian. He was born in 1577 and died around 1652, or shortly thereafter. A record of Zhang Hong's life is set out in Xu Mingshi's *Hengxi Lu* ("Annals of Hengxi"). From Xu's text, we learn that Zhang Hong lived in Hengxi, a town six and a half kilometers to the southwest of Suzhou (today's Huqiu subdistrict in Suzhou, Fig. 1-1). In his youth, Zhang Hong had studied in the hopes of entering the public service, but had little success in the official examinations. Forced to find another way to make his living, he turned instead to painting. Zhang Hong's works had all the richness of tradition, and yet were not constrained by traditional convention, winning him great artistic renown. His family was extremely poor, and his parents, siblings, and other poor relations all depended on Zhang Hong and his artistic ability to provide for them, often going from hand to mouth. Yet even so, when his purse strings were less tight, Zhang Hong would not part lightly with his paintings. Xu's description presents the image of a typical traditional artist: highly talented, but living in long-time poverty; selling his art to provide for life's necessities, but always keeping his pride and integrity.

Looking back at Zhang Hong's pictures, we may find sufficient cause for raising him from the

典型的传统画家形象：他画艺高超却贫困潦倒，以卖画为生而又崇尚气节。

回顾张宏的作品以及对他所做的种种观察，我们有充分的理由，将他从原来不受中国画史垂青的处境，提升并尊奉为卓越、具有原创性且作品极为引人入胜的画家。

张宏绘画的主题之一是实景山水。实景画是明代苏州画家擅长的画种。从沈周的时代起，苏州的绘画大家便一直在描绘城里城外的风光名胜或古迹。但就其特色而言，这些画作都极为程式化，景物之间的远近距离往往受到极端的压缩，为了将几处不同的地标放在一幅画作中，每件作品中的自然景致，都严格且毫无例外地屈

relative neglect he has suffered in China and regarding him as an excellent, innovative, quite fascinating artist.

Topographical paintings make up a significant portion of Zhang Hong's oeuvre. Such paintings were a specialty of the Suzhou School, and Suzhou masters from the time of Shen Zhou onward had been portraying notable scenes and monuments in and around the city. But they tended to be quite schematic in character, often telescoping distance radically to bring several landmarks into a single picture, and in all cases subjecting the scenery rigorously to the dictates of established style. Accommodations made to the particular visible features of the place, that is, were relatively few and, much of the time, consisted merely of adding identifying attributes to standard landscape types.

From the beginning, Zhang Hong's pictures of real places had broken with this pattern in important ways. He chose subjects that were not necessarily in the guidebook lists of notable sights of the region and painted them with an increasing disregard for precedent. Many of Zhang Hong's paintings are the products of first-hand observation, visual reports rather than conventional images (see e.g. Fig. 1-2). In depicting topographical scenes as seen directly by the eye, Zhang Hong came closer to a truly empirical approach to the representation of visual reality than any Chinese master had before. The critics of the time, as we might expect, were unable to deal with this aspect of his painting. "His hills and valleys are mysterious and unusual," writes one of them, adding irrelevantly: "He really captured the methods of the Yuan masters." Hills and valleys in painting that looked more than ever before like hills and valleys in nature must indeed have seemed strange and unusual.

Ernest Gombrich's well-known theory, according to which the artist begins with established artistic forms and gradually corrects them until they approximate the optical image, gives an apt encapsulation of the art-historical process that is loosely called "a return to nature", and seems particularly applicable to the development of Zhang Hong's style.

张宏与《止园图》

服在行之有年的绘画风格之下，任其处置。换言之，画家多半只在定型化的标准山水格式之中，附加一些可以令观者验证实景的地物罢了。

张宏的实景山水一开始便以重要的方式，打破了这种模式。他所选择的景致并不一定列在当地的名胜指南中，而他作画的方式也愈有推翻成规之势。张宏的许多画作，很明显是画家第一手的观察心得。可以说是视觉报告，而非传统的山水意象。当他在画中重现眼睛所见的实景时，他比任何一位传统大家都要更胜一筹，更能达到一种近乎视觉实证主义的境界。可以预期的是，对于张宏这样的作画态势，当时的画评并不知如何应对。

其中一位评家言其作品"丘壑灵异"，随后又天外飞来一句："得元人法。"与前人的作品相比，张宏画中的丘壑看起来更像自然真景，想必的确予人怪异之感吧 (Fig.1-2)。

贡布里希著名的理论告诉我们，艺术家在创作之初，系以行之有年的艺术形式入手，而后再一步步修正这些既有的形式，直到这些形式贴近视觉景象为止。就实景绘画"回归自然"的过程观之，贡布里希此一说法乃是较为真实的写照，同时，似乎也特别能够用来观照张宏画风的发展。

张宏虽然采取了较为直接的方式，将观察自然的心得，融入作画的过程之中，但这并非只是"应物象形"，而是创造一套刻画自然形象的新法则。画中对于细节的描述巨细靡遗，有时即使描绘一些我们并不熟悉的地方，仍能为作品注入一股超越时空的可信感。非但如此，张宏画中种种不同的物质形象，经过组合之后，形成鲜活有力的构图形式，使我们对于他笔下山景的宏伟气势，以及其在视觉上所造成的千变万化，备感印象深刻。

1627 年，张宏以止园为题，创作了一部多达二十页的画册。我对不同绘画形式及绘画目的的思考最后常常导向同一个结论：张宏的《止园图》是目前所能见到的最为真实生动地再现了中国园林盛时风貌的画作。

Fig. 1-2
(明) 张宏，《越中十景图》
(选二)，奈良大和文华馆藏
Two of the ten paintings from Zhang Hong's *Ten Scenes of Yue*. Held by the Museum of Japanese Art, Nara

这套图册到底有何非凡之处？我曾打过一个比方。请观者想象自己是一名园林专家，在阿拉丁神灯的帮助下，获允带上相机，跨越时空，回到一座古代园林中。观者可以从任何角度随意拍摄彩色照片，但有一个限制，狡猾的灯神在相机里只放了二十张胶片。此时，你会如何记录这座园林？

张宏的《止园图》正如同现代的相机记录，他抛弃了文人山水画的传统原则，甚至连册页的常规手法也未予理会。第一幅图画，他从今天用无人机才能拍摄到的视角，描绘了整座园林的鸟瞰全景。其后的 19 幅图画，则如同在园中漫步一般，沿着特定的游线拍摄照片，记

However, in bringing the observation of nature more directly into the artistic process, Zhang Hong is not merely "copying outer appearances" but creating a new order of natural images. The inclusion of particularising detail, even though it refers to places unfamiliar to us, gives his pictures a credibility that transcends time and place. Moreover, the varied materials of his painting are organized into fresh, strong compositions which impress upon us both the majesty and the visual multiplicity of the mountain scenery he portrays.

In 1627, Zhang Hong painted an album of twenty leaves with Zhi Garden as its subject. This was a very peculiar album, as it bore features not only of the album form, but also those of the handscroll and hanging scroll. Herein also lay my principal interest in Chinese garden painting — the different forms Chinese artists had used for their representations of gardens, and what features and aspects of the gardens they were able to convey in their representations. And considerations of these different forms and purposes always led to the same climactic ending: a presentation of Zhang Hong's *Zhi Garden Album* as by far the most visually informative record that we have of how a great Chinese garden, from the greatest period of the garden in China, really looked.

So what exactly is it that makes the *Zhi Garden Album* stand out? I once drew the following analogy — I asked viewers to imagine that they were Chinese garden specialists, and with the aid of Aladdin's lamp, were able to travel back in time to one of the great historic gardens with a color camera conveniently on hand. No limit is placed on the choice of vantage points, however, the crafty genie has only provided a twenty-exposure roll of film. How then would you, as the fortunate specialist, choose to record the garden?

Zhang Hong's paintings are like photographs from the genie's camera. He abandoned all traditional conventions of literati landscape painting, and even threw aside the accepted scheme of the album form. The first painting, *Panorama of Zhi Garden*, is from a vantage point that today would require a drone, and lays out the entire garden in full from a bird's eye view. The remaining nineteen are spatially interlocked as if they were photographs recording the progress of a leisurely stroll along a predetermined path, and together form a continuous and comprehensive vista. Not all of these have a central theme, some instead act as links that show where the different scenes depicted are positioned relative to each other. Each of the scenes presented in the nineteen subsequent paintings can also be located within the first painting of the bird's eye view. This careful and ingenious mode of pictorial exposition means that, when combined, the twenty leaves of the *Zhi Garden Album* reproduce both the overall schema as well as the defining details of the garden (Fig. 1-3).

At the same time, however, the paintings in the *Zhi Garden Album* are not merely photographic reproductions of views from chosen vantage points. Like all artists, Zhang Hong also had to undertake the process of selection and tailoring. And just like his orthodox literati counterparts, Zhang Hong drew his subject matter from nature. What differentiated them was that the literati artists reshaped natural landscapes so that they conformed to longstanding conventions of composition and style, whereas Zhang Hong made successive corrections to the existing conventions until they approached equivalence with visual observation.

Because he was so thorough, meticulous, and brilliantly effective, the source and origin of the techniques Zhang Hong used to create his works became almost irrelevant. The eyes and minds of his viewers are so entirely engaged with the content of the paintings that the existence of technique and convention is completely overlooked. Taking an entirely different path to Dong Qichang's insistence on having "no single brushstroke without a hallowed source", Zhang Hong opened up new possibilities in Chinese painting.

As its name suggests, the *Zhi Garden Album* is a series of paintings made in the leaflet/album format. Yet it is a very extraordinary album of leaflet paintings. While retaining the traditional

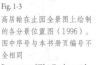

Fig. 1-3
高居翰在止园全景图上绘制的各分景位置图（1996）。图中序号与本书册页编号不全相同

Panorama of Zhi Garden, with the location of the scenes in the 19 successive paintings marked in by Cahill (1996). The order of paintings in the figure is Cahill's numbering and may not match the numbering of paintings in this book

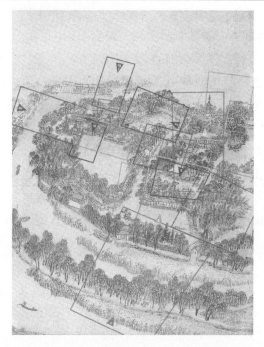

录下一系列连续的景致；这些图画，有些有居中的主景，有些则辨不出主景，而是描绘了景致间的关系。整套图册通过精心的编织，使各图景致都能与全景图的相关区域对应。如此一来，当它们合在一起时，既能从全局上，又能从细节上再现整座园林（Fig. 1-3）。

同时，《止园图》并非仅仅是框选景致并将它们如实画下，同所有画家一样，张宏也要经过剪裁和取舍。张宏与传统画家都是从自然中撷取素材，在这一点上他们并无不同。两者的区别在于：后者让自然景致屈服于行之有年的构图与风格，张宏则是逐步修正那些既有的成规，直到它们贴近视觉景象为止。由于他用心彻底，成果卓著，最终使得其原先所依赖的技法来源几乎变得无关紧要。观者的视界与精神完全被画中内容吸引，浑然忘却技法与传统的存在。跟董其昌的"无一笔无出处"相比，张宏选择了一条相反的道路，由此出发，开拓出中国绘画的另一种可能性。

从园林绘画的分类看，《止园图》属于册页，但却是一套不寻常的册页。《止园图》在继承册页传统的基础上，融合了手卷和单幅的优点：既像册页那样描绘了各处特定的景致，又像手卷那样将前后景致联系起来，并以单幅全景图来统摄各幅分景图，使整套图册成为有机的整体，手法纯熟而精到。

张宏选择了以具象再现作为创作的宗旨，他运用极具创意的斜景与截景构图，营造出俯视花园庭院时，得以窥视受遮蔽空间之内部的视效；并将线条与有似于点彩派画家的水墨、色彩结合起来，形象地描绘出各种易为人感知的形象。《止园图》中潋滟的池水、峥嵘的湖石以及枝叶繁茂的树木，使他笔下的景致具有了一种超乎寻常的真实感。

中国园林绘画历经上千年的演变，到明代达到顶峰，成为一类独立的画种。进入明代后，园林绘画受到北宋传统的影响和西洋风格的启迪，并与明代兴盛的造园活动交织互动，涌现出众多精彩的杰作。张宏《止园图》是这批杰作中的一颗明珠，它兼采中西的传统和技艺，取得了重大的突破和创新，不但打通了册页、手卷和单幅的界限，而且使园林、绘画和文学等诸多艺术完美交融。

张宏《止园图》不愧为明代园林绘画的"集大成之作"。

features of the leaflet/album, it also amalgamates the advantages of the handscroll and the hanging scroll. Zhang Hong's album not only provides detailed individual renderings of the various scenes and features of Zhi Garden, but also links each scene together to provide the continuity of the handscroll, and unites them all in a hanging scroll-like painting in which a full view of the entire garden is depicted, deftly integrating the album into an organic whole.

Zhang Hong aimed for representationalism as his artistic ideal, and employed highly innovative oblique views and cut-off compositions to produce the effect of gazing down into the sheltered interiors of the garden courtyards. His style combines lines with a Pointillist-like use of ink wash and color, creating vivid, easily perceptible images. The rippling water, striking rockeries, and verdant greenery in the *Zhi Garden Album* all serve to give an added degree of reality to the scenes he set to paper.

After a thousand or so years of evolution, Chinese garden painting came into its prime during the Ming dynasty, becoming a recognized category of painting in its own right. Developments in Chinese garden painting since the Ming dynasty were in turn influenced by previously abandoned traditions from the Song dynasty, by inspiration stimulated by the Occidental style of painting, and by the dynamic interaction of the art with the flourishing of garden building during this period. Unsurprisingly, the Ming dynasty saw the birth of many brilliant masterpieces. Zhang Hong's *Zhi Garden Album* is one of the brightest jewels amongst these masterpieces. It amalgamates the traditions and techniques of China and the West, achieving important breakthroughs and innovations. Not only does the album overcome the limitations of the leaflet/album, handscroll, and hanging scroll formats, it also accomplishes an organic fusion between the arts of painting, literature, and the garden.

As such, Zhang Hong's *Zhi Garden Album* represents a veritable epitome in Ming dynasty garden painting.

Preface:
Zhang Hong and the *Zhi Garden Album*

摘自高居翰《山外山》《气势撼人》
《不朽的林泉》
Extracted and rearranged from James Cahill's
The Distant Mountains, The Compelling Image,
and *Garden Paintings in Old China*

The Eternal Glade: Recreating a vanished great garden

林泉不朽，名园重现

The Museum of Chinese Gardens and Landscape Architecture in Beijing has two large-scale models that are amongst the finest works in its collection. Both are the exquisite work of master sculptors, made of rare and valuable materials, and both are also recreations of great historical gardens that have now since vanished. The first model is of the renowned Yuanming Yuan, the Old Summer Palace, which represents the crown jewel of classical Chinese royal gardens. The second is of Zhi Garden, once located in the city of Changzhou in Jiangsu Province, chosen as representing the archetypal private garden from the Jiangnan region, and in which we can see embodied the distinctive traits from the great age of gardens in the Ming dynasty.

Built in an earlier period than Yuanming Yuan, Zhi Garden, like many once-famous gardens, was consumed by the inexorable tides of time until it faded from memory. Fortunately, however, the *Zhi Garden Album* survived, and with it, a pictorial record of its namesake. Its leaves crossed the Pacific and the Atlantic, passing into the hands of various American and European collectors, serendipitously unlocking the secret of a long-forgotten past, and allowing Zhi Garden to be recreated for posterity.

This reclaiming of the past began with an American scholar's love of China.

In the turmoil of domestic unrest and foreign

北京的中国园林博物馆藏有两件园林巨雕模型，为馆藏中的精品。两件模型都由雕刻大师精心制作，用材珍贵，做工优良，再现了两座已经消失的历史名园。第一座是举世闻名的圆明园，代表了中国古代皇家园林的最高成就。第二座是明代常州止园，作为私家园林的代表，体现了明代造园盛世的艺术风范。

止园的年代比圆明园更为久远，然而却同许多名园一样，湮灭于时间长河之中，被人遗忘。幸运的是，描绘该园的《止园图》一直流传于世，它们漂洋过海，散落到国外。《止园图》曾多次转手，分藏在多处，辗转于欧美收藏家之手，意外地揭开了尘封的往事，让止园重现于世。

这一切还要从一位美国学者的中国情结说起。

他对《止园图》情有独钟，断言这套图册并非寻常的写意之作，而是描绘了一座真实存在过的园林，从而开启了寻找止园之旅。这位学者，就是著名的美国艺术史学家高居翰（Fig. 2-1）。

高居翰任教于加州伯克利大学，曾两次获得美国大学艺术学会的终身成就奖，2010 年获得美国史密森学会的弗利尔奖，是艺术史领域的权威学者。20 世纪 50 年代，高居翰首次在麻省剑桥看到张宏的《止园图》，立刻被

Fig. 2-1
高居翰绣像。孙燕云创作
Embroidered portrait of James Cahill. By Sun Yanyun

林泉不朽, 名园重现

画家独特的写实风格吸引。20 世纪七八十年代，他在哈佛大学的诺顿讲座和系列著作《气势撼人》《山外山》中，将《止园图》列为中国写实主义绘画的经典作品，确认了张宏在中国画史上的独特地位。

《止园图》共 20 幅，历经多次分合。1996 年高居翰联合收藏该图的洛杉矶郡立美术馆和柏林东亚艺术博物馆（今柏林亚洲艺术博物馆），举办了一场完整的《止园图》展，在国际上引起轰动。展览结束后，高居翰协助洛杉矶郡立美术馆购买到私人收藏的十二幅册页，其他八幅藏在柏林东亚艺术博物馆，都归公立机构所有，从此学者和公众可以更便利地接触到它们。

高居翰多次强调，《止园图》描绘的是一座真实存在的园林，如果深入研究，完全可以根据图册重建止园。然而，由于艺术史学者深受中国绘画崇尚写意的影响，高居翰又无法确定止园的园主和位置，因此一直无法说服人们相信止园的存在。

如果止园只是一座画家想象的园林，《止园图》并非根据实景创作，那么高居翰基于这套图册展开的理论建构，就不过是缺乏根基的空中楼阁。

1978 年园林学家陈从周应邀前往纽约，协助建造大都会美术馆的中国庭园"明轩"。这是中美文化交流史上的重要事件。高居翰在此期间拜访了陈从周，与他讨论《止园图》，并将 14 幅册页复制图片赠送给陈从周。

2004 年陈从周《园综》一书出版，收录了历代的 322 篇园记，成为研究中国园林最重要的文献集成。《园综》开篇刊登了高居翰赠送他的 14 幅《止园图》黑白图片，这是《园综》收录的唯一一套园林影像。《园综》是学者研习中国园林的必备图书，《止园图》由此进入园林学者的视野。

2010 年园林学家曹汛在中国国家图书馆发现《止园集》，为国内仅存的孤本（Fig. 2-2）。书中的园诗和园记

invasion during China's modern history, many works of Chinese art were lost and scattered overseas. The *Zhi Garden Album* was amongst these, changing hands many times, with its leaves separated and held in different collections. In the course of its journey, the album — more than once — passed through the hands of an American scholar who developed a particular fascination with its paintings. He asserted that the paintings collected in the album were not the usual works of expressionism commonly seen in Chinese art, but faithful depictions of a garden that had actually existed, and started on the quest of searching for Zhi Garden. This scholar was none other than the renowned art historian James Cahill (Fig. 2-1).

Cahill was a leading authority on art history. He taught at UC Berkeley, and was a two-time recipient of the College Art Association's Lifetime Achievement Award. In 2010, Cahill was awarded the Smithsonian Institution's Charles Lang Freer Medal, in recognition of a lifetime of seminal contributions to the field of art history.

Cahill first saw the *Zhi Garden Album* as a student in the nineteen fifties, in a museum in Cambridge, Massachusetts, and was immediately drawn by the unique realism of the artist's style. In both his 1979 Norton Lectures at Harvard (later published as *The Compelling Image*) and in *The Distant Mountains* (the third volume of his *History of Later Chinese Painting* series which he began in the same year), Cahill points to the *Zhi Garden Album* as a classic work of Chinese realist painting, cementing Zhang Hong's unique place in the history of Chinese art.

The *Zhi Garden Album* is made up of twenty leaves, which have been broken up and reunited multiple times in different groupings. In 1996, Cahill organized a collaboration between the Los Angeles County Museum of Art (LACMA) and the Museum für Ostiatische Kunst to reunite the twenty leaves of the *Zhi Garden Album* from their own and private collections, and present an exhibition of the album in its entirety. This was the first time that the full album could be viewed together since it was broken up almost

fifty years ago, garnering much attention from the international art community.

After the close of the exhibition, Cahill assisted the LACMA with the purchase of the twelve leaves from the *Zhi Garden Album* that were in private collections. This placed all twenty leaves of the album in the collection of public museums (the remaining eight being held by the Museum für Ostiatische Kunst in Berlin) making them readily accessible to researchers and the general public.

Cahill reiterated many times his assertion that the *Zhi Garden Album* depicted an actual historical garden, and with sufficient research, it would be entirely possible to reconstruct Zhi Garden based on the album's paintings. However, the prevailing view among art historians was that Chinese painting aimed for expressionism rather than realism, and Cahill did not have any way of determining who the owner of the garden was or where it was once located. Unsurprisingly, therefore, Cahill had little success in convincing people of his view.

If Zhi Garden existed only in the artist's imagination, and the *Zhi Garden Album* was not infact painted from real-world scenes, then the theoretical constructs that Cahill had developed around the album would be no more than empty claims without foundation.

In 1978, Chinese garden specialist Chen Congzhou traveled to New York to assist with the construction of the Met Museum's Chinese garden courtyard, Astor Court. This was a major milestone in Sino-American cultural exchange. It was also at this time that Cahill met with Professor Chen, engaging in academic discussions on the *Zhi Garden Album* with him, and gifting him with pictures of fourteen leaves from the album.

In 2004, Chen's book *Yuan Zong* ("A Compendium of Chinese Gardens") was published. This was an anthology that brought together 322 pieces of garden writing from various times in history, and which has since become one of the most important collections of literature for the study of Chinese gardens. In the opening pages before the main text, Chen reprints the fourteen black and white photos of the *Zhi Garden Album* paintings that Cahill had gifted to him. These are the only pictorial records included in *Yuan Zong*, a standard reference book for any scholar of Chinese gardens. Thus, in this way, the *Zhi Garden Album* found its way into the sights of Chinese garden scholars.

In 2010, Chinese garden historian Cao Xun discovered Wu Liang's *Zhi Yuan Ji* ("Zhi Garden Collection") in the National Library of China. This was the only existing copy of the book in the country (Fig. 2-2). The poem and prose descriptions in *Zhi Yuan Ji* matched the scenes illustrated in the *Zhi Garden Album*. From this, Cao concluded that the book's author, Wu Liang, was the owner of Zhi Garden, and that the garden itself was located in Wu Liang's hometown — the city of Changzhou in Jiangsu Province.

Cao was a student of Liang Sicheng, the father of modern Chinese architecture, and was himself a leading authority on Chinese architectural history and Chinese gardens. As only the fourteen leaves of the *Zhi Garden Album* reprinted in *Yuan Zong* were available to researchers in China at the time, Cao asked us to contact Cahill so that he could view the album in its entirety. An ocean away in America, Cahill was ecstatic to hear that the owner of Zhi Garden had been discovered, fulfilling a long-held ambition of his, and happily provided us with a full reproduction of the complete *Zhi Garden Album*. Along with the album, Cahill also sent us a copy of the Chinese garden paintings he had collected over the years, and proposed collaborating on a project on Chinese garden paintings. In 2012, *Garden Paintings in Old China*, the product of the work in which we aided Cahill, was published by SDX Joint Publishing Company. The first chapter of this book gave a detailed introduction to Zhi Garden, evoking keen interest from the fields of both Chinese garden studies and art studies.

Garden Paintings in Old China was the first published academic monograph, both in China and internationally, that gave a systematic

Fig. 2-2
吴亮《止园集》中的《止园集自叙》和《止园记》。中国国家图书馆藏
"Author's Preface" to *Zhi Yuan Ji* and "Impressions of Zhi Garden" from Wu Liang's *Zhi Yuan Ji*. Held by the National Library of China

恰与《止园图》对应，曹汛确定止园的主人便是文集的作者吴亮，止园位于吴亮的家乡——江苏常州。

　　曹汛师从梁思成先生，是中国建筑史、园林史研究的权威。当时国内只能见到 14 幅《止园图》，他委托我们与高居翰联系，以求图册的全貌。远在美国的高居翰听闻发现了止园的主人，多年的心愿变成现实，欣然寄来全套《止园图》的复制件。高居翰还一并寄来他历年收集的园林绘画图像，建议联合展开园林绘画研究。2012 年我们协助高居翰完成《不朽的林泉——中国古代园林绘画》，由三联书店出版。书中第一章详细介绍了止园，在园林学界和美术学界引起热烈的反响。

《不朽的林泉》是国内外首部系统探讨园林绘画的学术专著，随着影响的不断扩大，止园的故事越来越为人所知。作为罕见的能够根据图像复原全貌的明代园林，止园补足了中国园林史上的重要一页。为了让更多人直观地领略明代江南园林的风采，2015年中国园林博物馆决定制作止园模型，由非遗技艺传承人、微雕大师阚三喜负责，并邀请我们主持止园复原的学术研究，以求最大限度地重现名园风貌。

2017年止园模型在中国园林博物馆展出，20余平方米的巨大模型占据了整间展厅；同年出版的《消失的园林——明代常州止园》一书，介绍了从《止园图》到模型制作的完整过程。

由高居翰发起的止园研究，在中美学人和文博机构的携手努力下，不但确定了园主和园址，园林也以模型的形式重现人间，完成了从二维绘画向三维实体的跨越。

止园的传奇仍在继续。2018年春，宜兴博物馆馆长邢娟到中国园林博物馆参观，指出止园主人吴亮正是当代书画家吴欢的先祖。在吴欢珍藏的《北渠吴氏宗谱》中，我们找到了吴亮，是北渠吴氏第九世，吴欢的祖父吴瀛是第十九世。同样出现在宗谱中的，还有著名画家吴冠中的父亲吴炳泽，是第十八世。吴氏家族在清代、民国和新中国代有才人出，最著名的要属艺术大师吴祖光和评剧表演艺术家新凤霞，两人正是吴欢的父母。

2018年12月，中国园林博物馆和北京林业大学联合举办了"高居翰与止园——中美园林文化交流国际研讨会"。高居翰的女儿、学生，吴氏家族的后人，以及研究园林、绘画和相关艺术的中外学者汇聚一堂，共同纪念高居翰为国际文化交流做出的卓越贡献（Fig. 2-3）。

2019年10月，止园所在的常州策划举办了"止园归来"艺术展，邀请当地的艺术家采用乱针绣、烙铁画、斧劈石等非遗工艺，围绕止园展开艺术创作，迎接被遗忘的历史名园回到故乡。

discussion of Chinese garden paintings. As its influence gradually grew, the story of Zhi Garden also became more widely known. As one of the few Ming dynasty gardens that it was possible to completely reconstruct based on pictorial records, Zhi Garden fills an important gap in the history of Chinese landscape architecture.

In 2015, the Museum of Chinese Gardens and Landscape Architecture decided to build a model of Zhi Garden so that the style and elegance of Ming dynasty gardens from the Jiangnan region could be brought before a wider audience in a more direct and intuitive way. The model was built by intangible cultural heritage successor and master sculptor Kan Sanxi, who specializes in miniature carving. We were invited to oversee the research and help ensure that the model replicated the great historical garden as faithfully as possible.

In 2017, the model of Zhi Garden was officially exhibited for public display. At more than twenty square meters, the exquisite large-scale model takes up almost the entire exhibition hall. In the same year, we also published *A Garden of the Past: Zhi Garden in Ming Dynasty Changzhou*, which tells the story of Zhi Garden from the painting of the *Zhi Garden Album* to the completion of the model now exhibited in the Museum of Chinese Gardens and Landscape Architecture.

Through the efforts and support of Chinese and American scholars and institutions alike, the

research into Zhi Garden that was initiated by Cahill has borne fruit. Not only has the owner and original site of Zhi Garden been found, but the garden itself has also been resurrected in model form, taking it out of its two dimensional existence in ink and paper and restoring it to something closer to its original three-dimensional state.

The saga of Zhi Garden continues to this day. In the spring of 2018, Xing Juan, director of the City Museum of Yixing, visited the Museum of Chinese Gardens and Landscape Architecture. On her visit, she pointed out that Wu Liang was an ancestor of contemporary artist and calligrapher Wu Huan. We found Wu Liang in the *Family Records of the Wus of Beiqu* from Wu Huan's private library. Wu Liang was a ninth-generation descendent of the family, while Wu Huan's grandfather Wu Ying was of the nineteenth generation. Also appearing in the genealogy was Wu Bingze (of the eighteenth generation), father of the renowned artist Wu Guanzhong. The Wu family produced many persons of note during the Qing dynasty, the Republican period, and the early years of the People's Republic, the most famous of whom were the master scholar, dramatist, and calligrapher Wu Zuguang, and Pingju[1] artist Xin Fengxia — who, as it happens, are none other than Wu Huan's father and mother.

In December 2018, the Museum of Chinese Gardens and Landscape Architecture and Beijing Forestry University co-hosted *James Cahill and*

Fig. 2-3
由中国园林博物馆和北京林业大学联合举办的"高居翰与止园"国际研讨会。从左至右：任向东、柯一诺、周莹、曹汛、斯基普·肯·布朗、吴欢、萨拉·卡希尔、黄晓、洪再新、刘珊珊、孔纨

James Cahill and Zhi Garden international symposium co-hosted by the Museum of Chinese Gardens and Landscape Architecture and Beijing Forestry University.

Left to Right: Ren Xiangdong, Einor Cervone, Zhou Ying, Cao Xun, Skip Sweeney, Ken Brown, Wu Huan, Sarah Cahill, Huang Xiao, Hong Zaixin, Liu Shanshan and Kong Wan

The Eternal Glade:
Recreating a vanished great garden

1. A form of Chinese opera which originated in the city of Tangshan in Hebei Province during the late Qing dynasty. Pingju is believed to be one of the most popular forms of opera in China, second only to Peking Opera. Operas in the Pingju repertoire are predominantly stories of the virtuous and righteous triumphing over evil, and indeed it is from this content that its name was derived — the Chinese character "ping" (评) means literally "commentary" or "to pass judgement".

Zhi Garden — an international symposium on Chinese gardens and Sino-American Cultural Exchange. Cahill's daughter and students, Wu Liang's descendants, and researchers of Chinese art, Chinese gardens, and other related fields from both China and abroad, gathered together to celebrate Cahill's remarkable contributions to the cultural exchange between China and the US (Fig. 2-3).

In October 2019, the *Return of Zhi Garden* exhibition was held in Changzhou, the city that had once been its home. Local artists were invited to create pieces centered around Zhi Garden using disordered stitching embroidery, pyrography, Fupi stone bonsai, and other intangible cultural heritage techniques, to welcome Zhi Garden back to its home city.

The discovery of Zhi Garden and the investigation into its history has become a much-praised feat of international cultural exchange. An American art historian's lifelong devotion to the study of the *Zhi Garden Album*, and quest to find its real-world origins; the passion of Chinese scholars and cultural institutions for restoring and breathing new life into their traditional heritage, provided the compelling momentum that propelled the research steadily forward, allowing this great garden that was once kept alive only in paintings to be brought back in ways more closely resembling its original form. Today, the historical site of Zhi Garden has been rediscovered in Changzhou, a new model of the garden sits in Beijing, and the paintings of the *Zhi Garden Album* are held in the collections of museums in Los Angeles and Berlin. Further initiatives for international collaboration await. This is an opportunity for Chinese culture to be brought to the world, and also the weaving of a thread in the ongoing narrative of researchers working beyond borders to preserve the shared heritage of humanity.

Fig. 2-4
止园精雕模型，长 5.4 米，宽 4.4 米。中国园林博物馆藏
Full model of Zhi Garden, 5.4m×4.4 m, held in the Museum of Chinese Gardens and Landscape Architecture

　　止园的发现和研究历程，已成为国际学术交流的佳话。美国学者高居翰毕生心系《止园图》，追问止园的踪迹；中国学者和文博机构怀着对传统文化复兴的热情，不断将研究扎实向前推进，让这座画中名园越来越真实地呈现在世人面前。如今止园遗址和止园模型（Fig. 2-4）位于常州和北京，《止园图》分藏在美国洛杉矶和德国柏林，国际间的合作仍有待继续展开。这是优秀的中国文化走向世界的契机，也是一段各国学人共同研究和延续人类宝贵遗产的传奇。

吴亮止园：文人园林的里程碑

Zhi Garden: A paradigm of the literati garden

明代万历三十八年（1610）吴亮聘请苏州造园家周廷策，在家乡常州建造止园。

吴亮（1562—1624）又名吴宗亮，字采于，号严所，别号止园居士。万历二十九年（1601）他40岁考中进士，最终官至北京大理寺少卿（正四品）。

止园所处的晚明是文人园林的极盛时期。《园冶》的作者计成为吴亮四弟吴玄建造东第园，《长物志》作者文震亨的长兄文震孟为吴亮文集作序，止园出自"明代造园四大家"之一的周秉忠之子周廷策之手。作为明代的精品名园，止园是继王世贞弇山园之后，中国造园史上一座新的里程碑。

止园占地50多亩，其东有15亩田地，共65亩，规模巨大，分为东区、中区、西区和外区四部分。园中水面最多，占4/10，约20亩；土石次之，占3/10，约15亩；建筑第三，占2/10，约10亩；花木最少，约5亩，仅占1/10。（Fig. 3-1）

山、水、花木和建筑作为园林的四大要素，在晚明已经确定。人们多以此为标准品评园林，并热衷于为各要素排列名次。止园水第一、山第二、建筑第三、花木第四，自然远胜于人工，属于上乘之作。

时人评价止园"独以水胜"。此园靠近护城河，周围三河交汇，园内水体多样，有池、潭、塘、塈、溪、泽、渠、涧、沟、堑、峡、泉、河、濠、江、湖、岛、屿、矶、滩等20余种。由于园址较为平坦，较少瀑布等竖向水体，主要通过溪、涧、沟、渠等线式水体，联络起池、潭、塘、塈等面式水体，在水平向上构成通贯的连绵水系 (Fig. 3-2)。

《止园图》描绘水景的有16幅，描绘舟船的有9幅。它们是对江南水乡的提炼与再现，展示出蔚为大观的水景园特色。止园提供了多样的舟游体验——既有波光云影间的孤舟垂钓，也有浩荡长河中的一苇独航；舟船上的人物，或沧溟空阔，名士扣舷而歌；或幽塘采菱，仙媛芳姿婀娜，深得水居之雅韵 (Fig. 3-3)。

止园四要素里，山仅次于水。《止园记》称"土石

In 1610, the thirty-eighth year of the reign of Emperor Wanli of the Ming dynasty, Wu Liang commissioned Suzhou garden designer Zhou Tingce to build a garden for him in his hometown of Changzhou. This was later to become Zhi Garden.

Wu Liang (1562–1624), also called Wu Zongliang, took the courtesy name Caiyu, and also went by the noms de plume Yansuo and Zhiyuan Jushi (literally "Master of Zhi Garden"). In 1601, Wu Liang's fortieth year, and the twenty-ninth year of the reign of Emperor Wanli, he earned his third degree under the *keju* system of the official selection, attaining the title of *jinshi*. At the height of his official career, Wu Liang was appointed Deputy Chief Justice of the Court of Judicature and Revision (the highest court in Imperial China) in Beijing, an official of the fourth rank.

The late Ming dynasty, during which Zhi Garden was created, was the golden age of the literati garden. Zhi Garden itself amalgamates many accomplishments of literati garden design. And yet given the credentials of both its owner and its designer, this should perhaps come as no great surprise. Let us look first at the owner Wu Liang's connections: Ji Cheng, author of the earliest major Chinese treatise on garden design, the definitive *Yuan Ye* ("The Craft of Gardens"), designed Dongdi Garden for Wu Liang's fourth brother, Wu Xuan; Wen Zhenmeng, the eldest brother of Wen

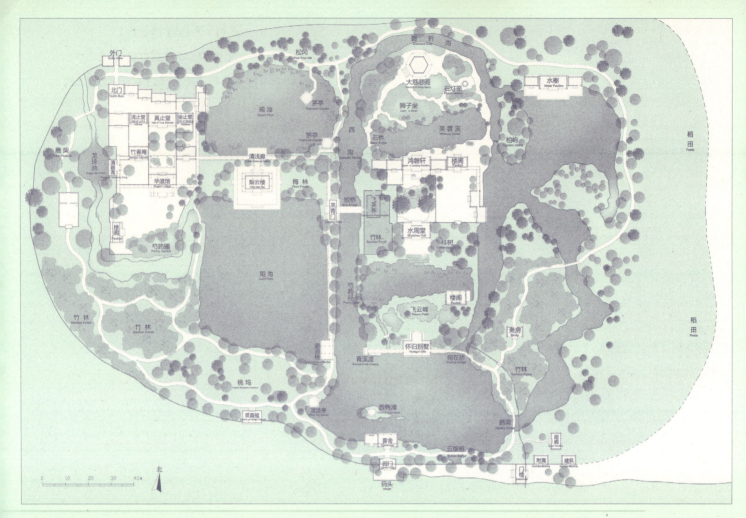

松冈
Pine Trees Hill

外门
Outer Gate

北门
North Gate

清止堂 真止堂 坐止堂
Hall of... Hall of True Stillness

竹香庵
清漪...

炯池
Quanli Pool

茅亭
Thatched Pavilion

茅亭
Hall of Grand Quietly

华滋馆
Huazi Hall

蹦折沼
Crescent Creek

大慈悲阁
Hall of Great Mercy

石灯笼
Stone Lantern

狮子坐
Lion's Seat

鹿柴
Deer...

龙坪池
Dragon Pool

梅林
Plum Forest

西沟
...

芙蓉溪
Hibiscus Creek

柏屿
Cypress Island

水榭
Water Pavilion

楼阁
Pavilion

清漪廊
Clear Shallows Gallery

梨云楼
Pear Blossom Tower

鸿鹈轩
Swan's Landing Pavilion

楼阁
Pavilion

芍药圃
Peony Garden

来青门
Laiqing Gate

板桥
Wood Bridge

飞英栋
...

水周堂
Shuizhou Hall

竹林
Bamboo Forest

稻田
Fields

楼阁
Pavilion

阻池
Jushi Pool

竹林
Bamboo Forest

竹林
Bamboo Forest

芍药圃
Peony Garden

飞云峰
Feiyun Peak

楼阁
Pavilion

怀归别墅
Huaigui Villa

竹林
Bamboo Forest

澍房
Study

稻田
Fields

桃坞
Peach Blossom Grove

青溪渡
Emerald Creek Crossing

宛在桥
Wanzai Bridge

竹林
Bamboo Forest

葆真楼
History of Heaven Tower

废波亭

教鸭滩
Duck Herding Beach

虹梁
Rainbow Bridge

水阁
Water Pavilion

建筑

喜舍

石版桥

园门

楼

附属

码头
Wharf

北
0 10 20 30 40

Zhenheng, author of *Zhangwu Zhi* ("Treatise on Superfluous Things")[2] wrote one of the prefaces to Wu Liang's *Zhi Yuan Ji*. Both these men were from the highest artistic circles of the time. The "lineage" of Zhi Garden is equally illustrious. Its designer was Zhou Tingce, son of Zhou Bingzhong, one of the four Ming dynasty "masters of the garden". A paradigm of Ming dynasty gardens and meticulously built by master craftsman, Zhi Garden represents, after Wang Shizhen's Yanshan Garden, yet another milestone in classical Chinese garden design.

Zhi Garden was built on a grand scale and covered an area of over 50 *mu* (or around three and one-third hectares — there are 15 *mu* to a hectare). To

Fig. 3-1

止园平面复原图。黄晓、王
笑竹、戈祎迎绘

Reconstructed plan of Zhi Garden. By Huang Xiao, Wang Xiaozhu and Ge Yiying

the east of the garden, there was also 15 *mu* of farmland, making up a total of 65 *mu*. This land was divided into the eastern, western, central, and outer zones (Fig. 3-1). Waterways took up the largest portion of the 50 *mu* garden, making up approximately four-tenths, or 20 *mu*, of the space. The next largest portion was taken up by landscaping and rock features, which accounted for approximately three-tenths, or 15 *mu*, of the garden space. Buildings and architecture made up the third-largest portion, accounting for approximately two-tenths, or 10 *mu*, of the area. Trees and plants made up the smallest portion, at around a tenth, or 5 *mu*, of the garden.

These four features — rockeries, water, plants, and architecture — had, by the late Ming dynasty, been confirmed as the four key elements of a garden. Rockeries, water, and plants were designated as natural or nature-like elements, while architecture was designated as an artificial element. These also formed the general criteria on which gardens at the time were judged, and it was common practice in critiques to assign a ranking to each element. In Zhi Garden, water ranked first, rockeries second, architecture third, and plants fourth. To use the language of Ming dynasty garden critiques, the natural elements in Zhi Garden far exceeded the artificial, making it a work of the highest order.

The distinguishing feature of Zhi Garden was its

2. Despite its name, the book is another definitive work on garden design, generally considered to be the equal and complement of *Yuan Ye*. Where *Yuan Ye* focuses on the building and design of a garden, *Zhangwu Zhi* focuses on the appreciation of the garden space.

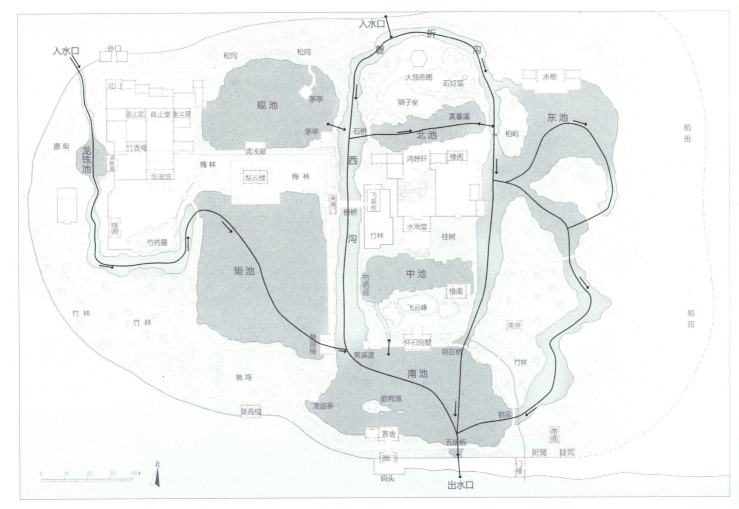

predominance of water. The garden was located at close quarters to the city moat, in a town situated near the junction where three rivers meet. These ample sources of water became a key asset in the creation of Zhi Garden. The garden boasted a wide and varied range of waterways and water features, including ponds, pools, lagoons, gullies, creeks, bayous, canals, brooks, dykes, moats, gorges, springs, streams, rivers, trenches, lakes, islands, cays, crags and beaches.

The land on which Zhi Garden was built was relatively level, without any changes in gradient. Thus waterfalls and other vertical water features appeared only a few far between. The entire waterway of the garden was like an interconnected web, with creeks, dykes, brooks and canals connecting pools, ponds, lakes and lagoons (Fig. 3-2).

The abundance of water in Zhi Garden can also be seen in the depictions made of it in the *Zhi Garden Album*, which contains sixteen paintings depicting waterscapes and nine which include boats or canoes. Zhi Garden's myriad waterscapes were a condensation and recreation of the "village on the waters" that typifies the Jiangnan region, creating a uniquely impressive wonderland of water — and also provided numerous venues for varied boating experiences. As Zhang Hong's album reveals to us, there were places for solitary fishing excursions amid the ripples of light and shade, and for journeys in a lone boat along the wide waters of a sweeping river. In these paintings, the characters on the boats range from sages relishing in the vastness of sky and water, to nymph-like maidens picking water lilies in a tranquil pond, adroitly portraying the joys of life on the water (Fig. 3-3).

After water, rockeries were the next most prominent of the four elements in Zhi Garden. Wu Liang wrote in *Zhi Yuan Ji* that Zhi Garden is made up of "three-parts landscaped earth and rockeries...and one-part forests of trees and bamboo". Thus rockery mountains and planted forests together took up four-tenths of the

Zhi Garden:
A paradigm of the literati garden

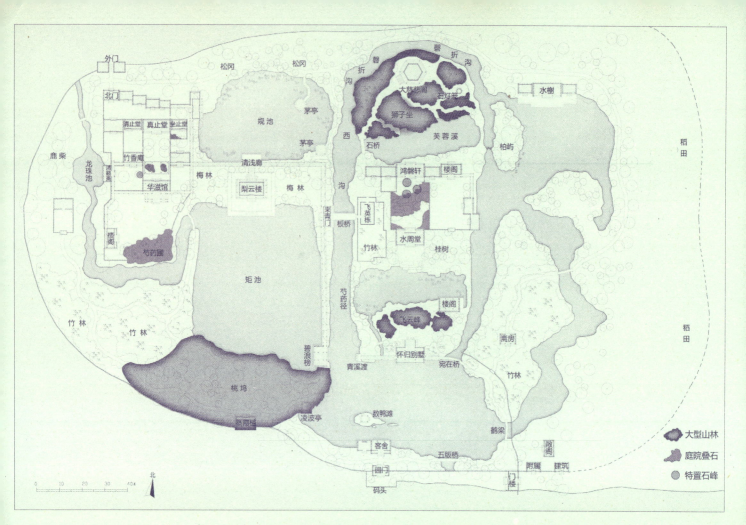

Fig. 3-4

止园叠山置石分布图。戈祎迎、
黄晓绘

3-4 Plan showing the distribution
of piled mountains and stone
arrangements in Zhi Garden.
By Ge Yiying and Huang Xiao

Fig. 3-5

《止园图》第十四开中的桃坞

Peach Blossom Harbour, detail
from Leaf 14 of the *Zhi Garden
Album*

三之，……竹树一之"。山与花木结合形成的"山林"，占到4/10，与水的比例相当。止园有大、中、小各种规模的叠山和置石，湖石山、黄石山、土山、石阶花台与特置石峰等，一应俱全（Fig. 3-4）。

大型山林有三组：一是中区南侧的桃坞，用池中挖出的泥土堆成，遍植桃树；与山体相比，桃坞的花木特色更为突出，以"林"取胜（Fig. 3-5）。二是东区北端的狮子坐，下部用土，上部堆筑黄石，山间栽种梧竹、梨枣、芙蓉等；这是一座土石山，植物较多，但仍呈露出粗犷的石质，山体以横向肌理为主，平稳敦厚，"山""林"构成平衡。三是怀归别墅北侧的飞云峰，以湖石垒叠，点缀一株孤松；这是一座全石假山，植物极少，山体玲珑，其竖向的挺拔之感，与狮子坐形成纵横的对比，以"山"取胜。

三组山林里飞云峰的堆叠难度最大，技术含量最高，最能体现周廷策的艺术成就。整座假山宛如从天外飞来，停落在四面环水的洲岛上。周围无山势可借，愈发加强了飞来之感。此山自带起峰和余脉，起自西南，收于东北，相连的芙蓉花台和狻猊怪石，有如飞来时散落

garden space, equal in area to the water surface of the garden. Zhi Garden had piled mountains and stone arrangements of all different scales, from the small, to the medium, to the very large, ranging in variety from Taihu stone rockeries, huangshi stone rockeries and earthen mountains, to stone steps, stone flower terraces, and standing stones (Fig. 3-4).

There were three large-scale groupings of "forest and mountain" in the garden. The first of these was "Peach Blossom Harbour" (*Taohua Wu*) in the south of the central zone. The "mountain" in this grouping was made using earth from the excavation of Juchi Pond,[3] with peach trees covering its slopes from foot to peak. Here, the trees are more striking and spectacular than the contours of the mountain itself, and prominence is given to forest over mountain (Fig. 3-5).

The second was the "Lion's Seat" (*Shizi Zuo*) at the north end of the eastern zone. The "seat" had an earthen base and an upper portion of piled huangshi stone, with bamboo, pear, red date, hibiscus, and parasol trees planted along its sides. Though quite heavily vegetated, the bones of the mountain could still be seen, their primarily horizontal veins visible and giving a sense of solid stability. Here, mountain and forest are in balance, each complementing the other.

The third was "Peak of Flying Clouds" (*Feiyun Feng*) on the north side of Huaigui Villa, made wholly of piled Taihu stone, and planted with a solitary pine. Its rising vertical lines contrast with the horizontal veins of the Lion's Seat, giving prominence to mountain over forest.

Of the three, the Peak of Flying Clouds was the most technically difficult, requiring the greatest skill and providing the greatest demonstration of Zhou Tingce's artistic genius. Modeled on Feilai

Feng ("Flying Peak") from Linyin Temple in Hangzhou, the Peak of Flying Clouds continues the tradition of "showing the grand through the miniature", which can be traced back to the Wei and Jin dynasties, and also embodies the new, late Ming philosophy of "the garden as painting". Artfully designed, the peak resembled a crag fallen from the sky to land on the water-bound island in Zhi Garden, an impression heightened by the absence of any surrounding slopes to lend their altitude. Rising in the southwest and flattening towards the northeast, its design incorporated a main peak and secondary ranges. The hibiscus terraces and peculiar stone arrangements that joined onto the peak mimicked the loose boulders that were scattered at the time of its landing. Together with a solitary pine and pavilion, the Peak of Flying Clouds was placed between Huaigui Villa and Shuizhou Hall, evoking the atmosphere of a dreamlike paradise (Fig. 3-6).

In addition to the three large scale recreations of mountains and forest, there were also four medium-sized rockeries of piled stone: the towering staircase in front of Swan's Landing Pavilion (*Hongpan Xuan*), the flower terrace of Taihu stone outside Huazi Lodge (Fig. 3-7), the arrangement of dramatically veined stone beneath the awnings of the Hall of True Stillness (*Zhenzhi Tang*), and the hillocks of earth and stone in front of the Hall of Resting Stillness (*Zuozhi Tang*). Numerous standing stones were also placed throughout the garden, including the Bharal Stone (*Qingyang Shi*) inside Swan's Landing Pavilion, Pincer Peak (*Xie'ao Feng*) and Buried Jade Pinnacle (*Yunyu Feng*) outside the pavilion, and the Stone of Classic Integrity (*Gulian Shi*) in front of Bamboo Convent (*Zhuxiang An*), adding interest to its many alcoves and spaces.

Finally, the buildings in Zhi Garden formed a counterpoint to the rockery mountains, waterways, and vegetation, creating an equilibrium between the man-made and the natural. Proportionately, architecture did not make up a large part of Zhi Garden, and yet in a sense, the buildings dominated their respective spaces (Fig. 3-8), reflecting conformity to the principle of balancing

Fig. 3-6
《止园图》第六开中的飞云峰
Feiyun Peak, detail from Leaf 6 of the *Zhi Garden Album*

3. The name of the ponds in the central zone of Zhi Garden — Guichi in the north and Juchi in the south — together form the phrase *guiju* (lit. "compass and square") meaning "rules" or "protocol", giving us another glimpse into the philosophy and ideals manifested in Zhi Garden.

Fig. 3-7

《止园图》第十六开中的芍药栏

Peony Wall (Shaoyao Lan), detail from
Leaf 16 of the *Zhi Garden Album*

Fig. 3-8

止园的建筑布局。黄晓、戈祎迎、
王笑竹绘

Plan showing the distribution of
buildings in Zhi Garden. By Huang
Xiao, Ge Yiying and Wang Xiaozhu

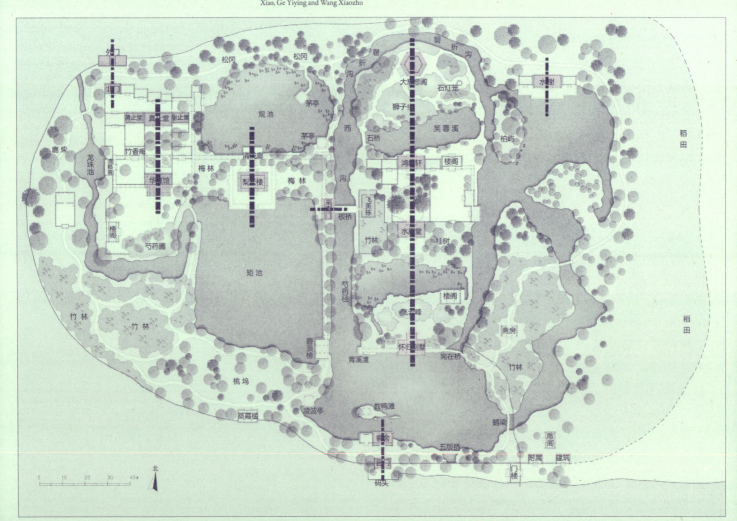

在周边的石块。这组山峰与孤松、楼阁相结合，安置在怀归别墅和水周堂之间，唤起观者梦幻十足的仙境想象。飞云峰模仿杭州飞来峰，继承了魏晋以来"小中见大"的叠山传统，并呼应了画意指导造园的晚明新风（Fig. 3-6）。

除了三组大型山林，止园还有四组中等规模的庭院叠石：一为鸿磐轩前"磊石为基，突兀而上"的石阶，二为华滋馆前的湖石花台（Fig. 3-7），三为真止堂前罗帐下的花石，四为坐止堂前的土石丘峦。此外还有多处特置的峰石，如鸿磐轩内的青羊石，轩前的蟹螯峰、韫玉峰，竹香庵前的古廉石，丰富了游园的趣味。

最后来看止园的建筑，与山、水、花木形成人工与自然的平衡。止园建筑的比重不高，但某种程度上却是各处空间的主宰，揭示了中国造园遵循的"奇正平衡"规则（Fig. 3-8）。

止园的东、中、西、外四区，都有主宰全区的主体厅堂，并形成明晰的轴线和游赏序列。东区南部以怀归别墅为主体，中部是水周堂和鸿磐轩，北部是大慈悲阁；

Fig. 3-9
止园中区主厅梨云楼
Pear Mist Hall, principal building in the central zone of Zhi Garden, detail from Leaf 12 of the *Zhi Garden Album*

外区以水轩为主体；中区以梨云楼为主体；西区前部和后部分别以华滋馆和真止堂为主体。各座建筑皆位于所在区域的中央偏北，面对主景，符合《园冶·厅堂基》"先乎取景，妙在朝南"的原则。合而观之，全园也有一座主体建筑，即中区的梨云楼，以巨大的规模和体量，丰富的借景和对景，彰显出"万物皆备于我"的主堂气魄（Fig. 3-9）。

止园以厅堂为主体，以门屋为辅助，确立起全园的主轴框架；其他建筑如东区的数鸭滩方亭、飞云峰东北的楼阁，中区的凌波亭、碧浪榜、蒸霞槛和规池的两座茅亭，西区的华滋馆西南楼阁和清籁斋等，则与溪池、

the "normal" (*zheng*) and the "extraordinary" (*qi*). The concept of *zheng* and *qi* comes from Sun-Tzu's *The Art of War*: "In battle, there are only the normal and extraordinary forces, but their combinations are limitless; none can comprehend them all."[4] *Zheng* and *qi* therefore encompass all the opposing dialectics that stem from the Chinese philosophy of the dynamic equilibrium of *yin* and *yang*, such as attack and defense, principal and secondary, the solid and tangible, and the empty and ethereal. Here, *zheng* represents the conventional rules of garden design, that give the garden order and regularity, while *qi* represents the breaking and modification of those rules, the flair and ingenuity that breathes vitality into the garden.

The eastern, western, central, and outer zones of Zhi Garden were each presided over by a principal building. This setup created a distinct axis and defined the order in which the various sections of the garden were to be visited.

In the eastern zone of the garden, Huaigui Villa reigned in the south, Shuizhou Hall and Swan's Landing Pavilion presided over the central region, and the Pavilion of Great Mercy dominated the north. The principal building of the garden's outer zone was the water pavilion, while the central zone had Pear Mist Hall as its primary architectural feature. In the western zone, Huazi Lodge and the Hall of True Stillness were the principal buildings of the north and south sections respectively.

Each of these principal buildings was placed slightly north of center in the section they presided over, and commanded views of the primary attraction in that region. This accords with the design principle in *Yuan Ye* that "the first consideration in determining location is the appeal of the vista it commands; this satisfied, principal buildings should ideally face south."

When the four zones are viewed as a whole, one also discovers that there was a building that was given primacy over all others — the principal building of the garden itself. This was Pear Mist Hall in the central region (Fig. 3-9). Grand and

Zhi Garden:
A paradigm of the literati garden

4. Sun-Tzu, *The Art of War* (Samuel B. Griffith trans, Oxford University Press 1971) p. 92 [trans of: 孙子兵法].

spacious, with rich vistas of borrowed scenery and viewing points that also doubled as views, it exuded the proud majesty of a principal hall that possesses all things complete unto itself.

The principal buildings of formal halls, accompanied by their auxiliary gatehouses, establish the overall layout of Zhi Garden, which embodies a *zheng* or conventional organization, with its features of regularity, order, and a clearly defined axis. The remaining buildings are organized following the philosophy of *qi*, or inventive freedom. For instance, Counting Duck Beach Pavilion (*Shuyatan Fangting*) and the pavilion at the northeast corner of the Peak of Flying Clouds in the eastern zone; Billow Top Gazebo (*Lingbo Ting*), Emerald Wave Pavilion (*Bilang Bang*), the Gallery of Gilded Clouds (*Zhengxia Jian*) and the two thatched pavilions in the waters of Guichi Pond in the central zone (Fig. 3-10); the southwestern wing of Huazi Lodge and the Studio of Heavenly Song (*Qinglai Zhai*) in the western zone; all of these were placed to set-off their surroundings. Whether overlooking the waters of stream or pond, sitting atop hills and islands, or peeking between tree and flower, the ingenious placement of these buildings adds dynamism to the ordered regularity of Zhi Garden, giving a vibrant spark of life to each section of the garden.

Zhi Garden takes its name from the lines

> *Then it was that I first found it good to put all things down*
>
> *And from this day on, true stillness shall be my resting place and refuge* [5]

from Tao Yuanming's [6] poem *Putting Down the Cup* ("Zhi Jiu"), and sets the overarching theme for the design of the garden. Through careful selection and clever referencing of Tao Yuanming's poetry, the designer creates a clear thread that links together all the main places of interest, embedding a narrative scheme into the design of Zhi Garden (Fig. 3-11). The main path of the narrative starts at the willow at the garden gate — an allusion to the *Biography of the Gentleman of the Five Willows* ("Wuliu Xiansheng Zhuan"), and is carried

丘岛以及花木配合，穿插掩映，随宜布置，营造出生机勃勃、富于变化的园林空间（Fig. 3-10）。

止园名称取自陶渊明的《止酒》诗，"始觉止为善，今朝真止矣"；继而精选诗情用典，以明晰的主线串联起各景，完成全园的叙事建构。止园以入口的柳树为起点，呼应陶渊明的《五柳先生传》；以怀归别墅和飞云峰的孤松为承接，呼应陶渊明的《归去来兮辞》和其中的"抚孤松而盘桓"；再以梨云楼和桃坞为转折，全园的主堂梨云楼对着象征桃花源的桃坞；最后是出自《止酒》诗的真止堂、坐止堂和清止堂。这四段景致皆围绕陶渊明展开，层层推进，同时辅以其他典故，使止园既主旨明确、

Fig. 3-10
止园中区规池中的茅亭
Thatched pavilion in Guichi Pond, detail from Leaf 13 of the *Zhi Garden Album*

脉络清晰，又摇曳多姿、意蕴丰富，俨成一篇匠心独运的绝妙文章，描画出一座远离尘嚣的桃花源（Fig. 3-11）。

5. This translation is based on Wu Liang's likely reading of these lines, given his retirement from office and subsequent life of semi-reclusion. A version more expressive of Tao Yuanming's intentions is as follows: "Then it was that I first found that abstinence was good/ And from this day on I vow to truly put down the cup".

6. Tao Yuanming (365-427), also called Tao Qian, was one of China's greatest poets and a noted recluse. He is regarded as the foremost representative of what is now known as "fields and gardens" or *tianyuan* poetry, and is known for the authenticity and spontaneity of his verse. In addition to his poetry, Tao is also famous for

resigning a secure government post (to avoid the taint of excessive formality and corruption of official life) and returning home to his garden to maintain his moral integrity. Tao's example of semi-reclusion in a garden was held to be a lofty ideal by the upper echelons and literati of the Ming dynasty.

forward by Huaigui Villa and the lone pine on the Peak of Flying Clouds — the former echoing the Chinese title of *Returning Home* ("Guiqu Laixi Ci") and the latter a physical manifestation of the final line in the second stanza of the same poem: "I walk around a lonely pine tree, stroking it."[7] The narrative then reaches its climax at Pear Mist Hall, which, as the principal building of Zhi Garden, sits opposite Peach Blossom Harbour, a representation of the utopia in *Peach Blossom Spring* ("Taohua Yuan").[8] Finally, the narrative closes with the Hall of True Stillness[9] (*Zhen Zhi Tang*), the Hall of Resting Stillness (*Zuo Zhi Tang*), and the Hall of Lyrical Stillness[10] (*Qing Zhi Tang*), all of which have names derived from lines in *Putting Down the*

Cup. The scenery in these four sections of the garden is also themed around Tao Yuanming and his poetry, progressively unfolding while also being augmented by allusions to other sources. Thus hidden in the frames and scenes of Zhi Garden is a singularly imaginative story, its leading theme distinctive and coherent, yet at the same time interspersed with variations, metaphors, and profound allusions. In building Zhi Garden, Wu Liang created for himself a world apart from the mundane, a Garden of Eden akin to Tao Yuanming's Peach Blossom Spring.

Fig. 3-11
止园布局谋篇的起承转合
Plan of Zhi Garden by narrative section

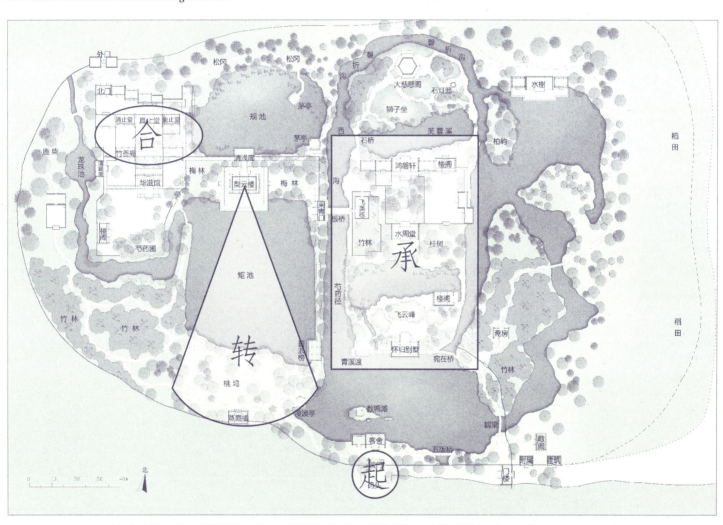

Zhi Garden:
A paradigm of the literati garden

---

7. Translation from James Hightower, *The Poetry of T'ao Ch'ien* (Oxford: Clarendon Press, 1970), pp. 269-270.

8. *Peach Blossom Spring* is one of Tao Yuanming's most representative works. It tells the tale of a fisherman who, following a stream lined with blossoming peach trees, stumbles upon an idyllic community that for generations has been sequestered from political and social upheavals. This bucolic world was a stark contrast to the society that Tao lived in, which was marked by political instability and national disunity. The term "Peach Blossom Spring" in Chinese came to symbolize an ideal world in which man lived in perfect harmony both with each other and with nature, an

Oriental version of the Western Arcadia.

9. Or, in the context of the poem, "true cessation", expressing Tao Yuanming's determination to commit to abstinence (this time!).

10. Or "eternal radiance" in the context of the poem, where the poet uses the replacement of his former aged features with the fresh face of eternal youth as an analogy to express his commitment to change his ways. Both the Hall of Lyrical Stillness and the Studio of Heavenly Song are built beside and take their names from the bamboo forest in Zhi Garden. The "heavenly song" is the sound of the bamboo leaves in the wind,

and the "lyrical stillness" is the silence that follows after the final note of music ends.

The Wus of Beiqu: A family of letters with long-standing heritage

吴亮出自宜兴北渠吴氏，为第九世，他的祖父吴性迁居常州洗马桥，因此又属于洗马桥吴氏。

止园只是吴氏众多园林中的一座，这个明清时期的造园世家，目前有记载的园林已发现 30 余座 (Fig. 4-1)。

吴亮的祖父吴性中嘉靖十四年 (1535) 进士，在常州建造了城隅草堂和天真园。

吴性育有五子。长子吴诚早卒。次子吴可行中嘉靖三十二年 (1553) 进士，继承了父亲的城隅草堂，并在宜兴滆湖建造沙滆湖居，在荆南山建造荆溪山馆。第三子

Wu Liang was of the ninth generation of the Wus of Beiqu Village in the city of Yixing. Wu Liang's grandfather, Wu Xing, moved his family to Ximaqiao in the city of Changzhou, and thus he is also of the Wus of Ximaqiao.

Wu Liang's Zhi Garden was only one of the Wu family's many gardens. To date, researchers have discovered over 30 of the gardens recorded as being built by this garden building family of the Ming and Qing dynasties (Fig. 4-1).

Wu Liang's grandfather Wu Xing, who instigated the migration of his branch of the family to Changzhou, attained his *jinshi* degree in the fourteenth year of the reign of Emperor Jiajing (1535). He built Parapet Villa (*Chengyu Caotang*) and the Garden of Unblemished Nature (*Tianzhen Yuan*) in his newly chosen home city.

Wu Xing had five sons. His eldest son Wu Xian died before adulthood. His second son Wu Kexing attained his *jinshi* degree in the thirty-second year of the reign of Emperor Jiajing (1553). Wu Kexing inherited Parapet Villa from his father, and also built Shagehu Lodge on Gehu Lake and Jingxi Mountain Villa in Jingnan Mountain (both in Yixing). Wu Xing's third son Wu Zhongxing attained his *jinshi* degree in the fifth year of the reign of Emperor Longqing (1571). He lived a life of seclusion in the countryside near Yixing, residing first for a time in Zengshan Mountain and

吴氏家族：
千古文心，书香一脉

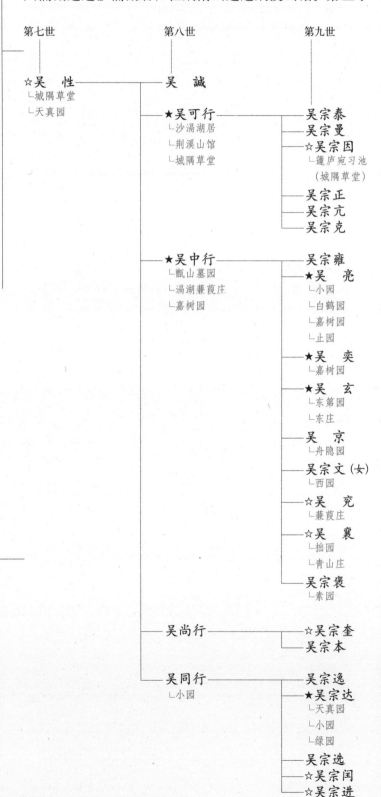

第七世　　　　　　第八世　　　　　　第九世

☆吴 性
└城隅草堂
└天真园

　　吴 诚

★吴可行
└沙滆湖居
└荆溪山馆
└城隅草堂

　　吴宗泰
　　吴宗曼
　　☆吴宗因
　　　└篷庐宛习池
　　　（城隅草堂）
　　吴宗正
　　吴宗亢
　　吴宗克

★吴中行
└甑山墓园
└滆湖蒹葭庄
└嘉树园

　　吴宗雍
　　★吴 亮
　　　└小园
　　　└白鹤园
　　　└嘉树园
　　　└止园
　　★吴 奕
　　　└嘉树园
　　★吴 玄
　　　└东第园
　　　└东庄
　　吴 京
　　　└舟隐园
　　吴宗文（女）
　　　└西园
　　☆吴 兖
　　　└蒹葭庄
　　☆吴 襄
　　　└拙园
　　　└青山庄
　　吴宗褒
　　　└素园

吴尚行
　　☆吴宗奎
　　吴宗本

吴同行
└小园
　　吴宗逸
　　★吴宗达
　　　└天真园
　　　└小园
　　　└绿园
　　吴宗选
　　☆吴宗闰
　　☆吴宗进

吴中行中隆庆五年（1571）进士，先后在宜兴甑山和滆湖隐居，并在常州北郊建造嘉树园。第四子吴尚行造园情况不明。幼子吴同行在常州建造小园。

吴氏造园的极盛期出现在吴亮这一辈。吴可行第三子吴宗因继承了城隅草堂，并拓建改筑为篸庐宛习池。吴同行第二子吴宗达继承了天真园，并新建了绿园。吴宗达（1575—1635）字上于，号青门，中万历三十二年（1604）探花，历任礼部尚书、东阁大学士、文渊阁大学士和建极殿、中极殿大学士等，是明清北渠吴氏功名

then on Gehu Lake, and built Jiashu Garden in the northern outskirts of Changzhou. There are no known records on the garden building activities of Wu Xing's fourth son Wu Shangxing. His youngest son Wu Tongxing built Xiaoyuan Garden in Changzhou.

Garden building in the Wu family reached its height in Wu Liang's generation. Wu Kexing's third son, Wu Zongyin, inherited Parapet Villa, which he expanded and rebuilt into Wanxi Pond Manor (*Julu Wanxi Chi*). Wu Tongxing's second son, Wu Zongda, inherited the Garden of Unblemished Nature and also built Lyuyuan Garden. Wu Zongda (1575 – 1635) took the courtesy name Shangyu and the nom de plume Qingmen. He placed third in the national *keju* examinations held in the thirty-second year of the reign of Emperor Wanli (1604), winning the title of *tanhua*. His official career included appointment as the Head of the Ministry of Rites, Grand Secretary of the Eastern Library, Grand Secretary of Jianji Hall, and Grand Secretary of Zhongji Hall ("Grand Secretary" was the equivalent of an advisor to the emperor, or a modern-day cabinet minister), making him the most illustrious member of the Wus of Beiqu in the Ming and Qing dynasties.

Wu Zhongxing had eight sons and one daughter. His eldest son Wu Zongyong died at 33. His second son, Wu Liang, was not only the creator of Zhi Garden, but also had a hand in some other gardens commissioned by the family, these being Xiaoyuan Garden, White Crane Garden, and Jiashu Garden. His third son, Wu Yi attained his *jinshi* degree in the thirty-eighth year of the reign of Emperor Wanli (1610), and undertook the rebuilding of Jiashu Garden, expanding the garden to its later scale. Wu Zhongxing's fourth son, Wu Xuan attained his *jinshi* degree in the twenty-sixth year of the reign of Emperor Wanli (1598). Of the eight brothers, Wu Xuan rose highest in government, holding the post of Right Commissioner of the Provincial Administration Commission of the Huguang Region (a sub-second rank official) at the peak of his career. He was the creator of Dongdi Garden and Dongzhuang Estate. Wu Zhongxing's fifth son

The Wus of Beiqu:
A family of letters with long-standing heritage

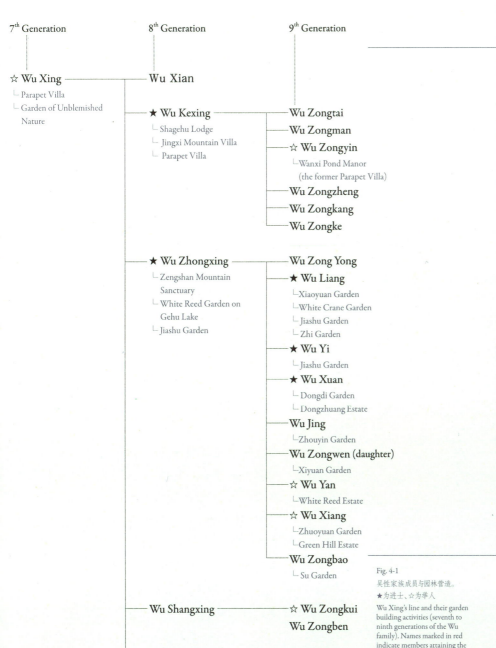

7th Generation	8th Generation	9th Generation
☆ Wu Xing	Wu Xian	
└ Parapet Villa		
└ Garden of Unblemished Nature		
	★ Wu Kexing	Wu Zongtai
	└ Shagehu Lodge	Wu Zongman
	└ Jingxi Mountain Villa	☆ Wu Zongyin
	└ Parapet Villa	└ Wanxi Pond Manor (the former Parapet Villa)
		Wu Zongzheng
		Wu Zongkang
		Wu Zongke
	★ Wu Zhongxing	Wu Zong Yong
	└ Zengshan Mountain Sanctuary	★ Wu Liang
	└ White Reed Garden on Gehu Lake	└ Xiaoyuan Garden
	└ Jiashu Garden	└ White Crane Garden
		└ Jiashu Garden
		└ Zhi Garden
		★ Wu Yi
		└ Jiashu Garden
		★ Wu Xuan
		└ Dongdi Garden
		└ Dongzhuang Estate
		Wu Jing
		└ Zhouyin Garden
		Wu Zongwen (daughter)
		└ Xiyuan Garden
		☆ Wu Yan
		└ White Reed Estate
		☆ Wu Xiang
		└ Zhuoyuan Garden
		└ Green Hill Estate
		Wu Zongbao
		└ Su Garden
	Wu Shangxing	☆ Wu Zongkui
		Wu Zongben
	Wu Tongxing	Wu Zongyi
	└ Xiaoyuan Garden	★ Wu Zongda
		└ Garden of Unblemished Nature
		└ Xiaoyuan Garden
		└ Lüyuan Garden
		Wu Zongxuan
		☆ Wu Zongrun
		☆ Wu Zongjin

Fig. 4-1

吴性家族成员与园林营造。
★为进士、☆为举人

Wu Xing's line and their garden building activities (seventh to ninth generations of the Wu family). Names marked in red indicate members attaining the *jinshi* degree, names marked in blue indicate members attaining the *juren* degree

Wu Jing built Zhouyin Garden. His sixth son Wu Yan attained his second, or *juren*, degree under the *keju* system of official selection in the twenty-eighth year of the reign of Emperor Wanli (1600), and built White Reed Estate. His seventh son Wu Xiang attained his *juren* degree in the nineteenth year of the reign of Emperor Wanli (1591), and built Zhuoyuan Garden and Green Hill Estate. Wu Zhongxing's eighth son Wu Zongbao built Suyuan Garden. His daughter Wu Zongwen married Cao Shirang, built Xiyuan Garden. In the generation that followed, Wu Zesi built Fragrant Snow Manor (*Xiangxue Tang*) and Wu Xiaosi built the Manor of Four Snows (*Sixue Tang*), continuing the family's long-lived tradition.

The gardens built by the Wu family in the Ming and Qing dynasties were not only remarkable for their number, but also noted for the fineness of their design, workmanship, and beauty. Qing dynasty author Tang Jianye wrote in his *Chronicles of Piling* ("Piling Jian Wen Lu") that

> There are four famous gardens in the seat of the prefecture, [Changzhou], Yangyuan Garden in the city's north-eastern corner, Green Hill Estate in its northern outskirts, and White Reed Estate and Crane's Rest Estate outside the lesser southern gate, all of which were estates of the Wus of Beiqu in the former Ming dynasty.

Three Wu family gardens are worthy of particular mention. The first is Wu Liang's Zhi Garden, which was a benchmark in Ming dynasty literati garden creation. The second is Dongdi Garden, which belonged to Wu Liang's fourth brother, Wu Xuan. Created by Ji Cheng, Dongdi Garden has long since been known to modern-day researchers. It was the work that propelled him into fame as a designer, and also features in his definitive work, *Yuan Ye*. The third is Green Hill Estate, which belonged to Wu Liang's seventh brother Wu Xiang. Green Hill Estate was also known in Changzhou as *Daguan Yuan*, or Grand View Garden. Covering a vast area of land and featuring a wealth of varied and captivating prospects, it was highly celebrated during the Ming and Qing dynasties, and featured in the poetry of respected scholars and poets such

最显赫的人物。

吴中行育有八子一女。长子吴宗雍早卒。次子吴亮除了建造止园，家族里的小园、白鹤园和嘉树园，都曾经其手。第三子吴奕中万历三十八年（1610）进士，拓建改筑嘉树园，奠定其规模。第四子吴玄中万历二十六年（1598）进士，官至从二品的湖广布政使司右布政使，在吴中行八子中官职最高，建有东第园和东庄。第五子吴京建有舟隐园。第六子吴亢中万历二十八年（1600）举人，建造了蒹葭庄。第七子吴襄中万历十九年（1591）举人，建造了拙园和青山庄。第八子吴宗褒建有素园。女儿吴宗文嫁曹师让，筑有西园。下一辈中吴则思有香雪堂、吴孝思有四雪堂，名门风雅，余韵不绝。

明清吴氏园林不但数量众多，而且质量上乘。清代汤健业《毗陵见闻录》评价道："郡城内有名园四：城东北隅为杨园，北郊为青山庄，小南门外为蒹葭、来鹤庄，皆前明北渠吴氏别墅。"他列举了四座常州名园，在明代全部属于吴氏。

吴氏园林有三座特别值得一提。除了吴亮止园，第二座是吴亮四弟吴玄的东第园，很早就被现代学者所知。东第园出自计成之手，计成通过此园一举成名，并将东第园写入造园名著《园冶》中。第三座是吴亮七弟吴襄的青山庄，在常州有"大观园"之称，占地广阔，造景丰富，明清之际盛极一时，大学者赵翼、洪亮吉、袁枚都曾慕名游览。

与园林兴盛相表里的是吴氏家族的人才辈出。仅从吴性到吴亮之子的四代人，吴氏便有12名进士和19名举人，在朝中及各地任官。洗马桥吴氏崛起为晚明江南的名门望族。

明清易代之际，江南望族大多遭到冲击。吴氏家族亦难逃人丁凋零、园亭荒废的命运，曾经的辉煌埋没到故纸堆中，以至后人亦鲜有知晓。然而，家族的生命活力并未磨灭。近现代时期，吴氏再次崛起，在文化、艺术、政治、军事诸领域做出了非凡的贡献。

艺术大师吴祖光是吴中行第十二世孙，属于北渠吴氏第二十世。他19岁创作出话剧《凤凰城》，赢得"戏剧神童"的美誉；后来又创作出《正气歌》《风雪夜归人》《林冲夜奔》《牛郎织女》和《少年游》等剧作，名震剧坛。吴祖光的妻子新凤霞是中国评剧最大流派——新派艺术的创始人，被誉为"评剧皇后"。吴祖光、新凤霞合作的《刘巧儿》《花为媒》《新凤霞传奇》，在中国产生了深远而广泛的影响（Fig. 4-2）。吴祖光的弟弟吴祖强是著名作曲家，曾担任中央音乐学院院长、中国音乐家协会副主席和中国文联执行副主席等职务，与吴祖光合誉为共和国文化艺术界的"双璧"。

as Zhao Yi, Hong Liangji, and Yuan Mei.

This profusion of garden building was an indirect reflection of the accomplishment of the family and its members. In four generations alone, starting with Wu Liang's grandfather and going down to Wu Liang's son, the family produced twelve members who attained the *jinshi* degree and nineteen who attained the *juren* degree. These family members went on to become officials in the imperial court, or various levels of government across the country. In the late Ming dynasty, the Wus of Ximaqiao became one of the most influential families of the Jiangnan region.

During the tumultuous time of dynastic transition between the Ming and Qing dynasties, almost all of the prominent families in Jiangnan suffered strife and upheaval. The Wu family was no exception, and were not spared the fate of having once-grand estates fall into disrepair, and a once populous household reduced and scattered to the four corners, its former glory buried in forgotten papers, rarely recalled in later generations. Yet the spark and brilliance of the family line had not died out, and the Wus again rose to prominence in modern and contemporary times, making extraordinary contributions in fields including arts and culture, politics, and military affairs.

The literary and artistic maestro Wu Zuguang, for

example, was a twelfth generation descendent of Wu Zhongxing (Wu Liang's father), and belongs to the twentieth generation of the Wus of Beiqu. He wrote the wartime drama *Phoenix City* at only nineteen, earning him repute as a prodigy playwright. Wu Zuguang went on to write *The Soul of China, Homecoming on a Snowy Night, The Flight of Lin Chong, The Cowherd and the Weaver Girl,* and *The Journey of Youth,* all of which were influential plays at the time, winning him great acclaim in theatrical circles. His wife, Xin Fengxia, was the creator of what is now the most widely performed style of Pingju Opera — the "opera nouveau" or new style Pingju, and was herself known as "the Queen of Pingju". The couple (Fig. 4-2) also collaborated to produce *Liu Qiao'er, The Floral Token,* and *The Legend of Xin Fengxia,* works of stage and screen that had a wide and profound impact in the newly formed People's Republic.

Wu Zuguang's younger brother, Wu Zuqiang, is a well-known composer. He was the former Dean of the Central Conservatory of Music, former executive vice-chairman of the China Federation of Literary and Art Circles, and has now been named honorary chairman of the Chinese Musicians' Association (having previously served as vice-president). The brothers are known as the new republic's twin stars of art and culture.

Going back one generation further, Wu Ying, the father of Wu Zuguang and Wu Zuqiang, represented the government in the acceptance of the Forbidden City, and was one of the founders of the Palace Museum. Following the Mukden Incident, historical artifacts from the Palace Museum were transported south. Wu Ying was head of the transport escort, and devoted tireless energy to the protection of these important artifacts. Wu Ying's father, Wu Lin, had served as an aide to Zhang Zhidong, one of the foremost reformers of the late Qing dynasty. During this time, Wu Lin presided over the restoration of the Yuewang Temple in Wuchang , promoting Yue Fei's[11] legacy of service and loyalty to his country. Wu Lin's father, Wu Yousun, assisted Zhang Zhidong with the establishment of the Hubei Military Academy and the training of the new troops, shaping the Hubei

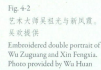
Fig. 4-2
艺术大师吴祖光与新凤霞。
吴欢提供

Embroidered double portrait of Wu Zuguang and Xin Fengxia. Photo provided by Wu Huan

The Wus of Beiqu:
A family of letters with long-standing heritage

11. Yue Fei (1103-1142) was one of China's greatest generals and is best known for leading the Southern Song forces in the wars against the Juchen-ruled Jin dynasty in northern China, which had taken the former Song dynasty capital of Kaifeng. He prevented the advance of the Juchen and was able to recover and secure some of the occupied territories in central China south of the Yangtze and Huai rivers. However, his attempt to push north and recover all the lost Song territories was opposed, and Yue Fei was imprisoned under concocted charges in 1141 and executed early the next year. According to historical records and legend, Yue Fei had the four Chinese characters *jing zhong bao guo* (精忠报国), meaning "serve the country with the utmost loyalty", tattooed across his back – words which now serve as an encapsulation of his spirit and character.

New Army into one of the most combat-effective units in the late Qing military.

Wu Zuguang's line of the family came from the branch that had migrated to Changzhou — the Wus of Ximaqiao. Yet another world-class modern-day artist was also born into the Wu family, in their ancestral home of Beiqu Village in Yixing — painter and educator Wu Guanzhong, a nineteenth-generation descendent of the Wus of Beiqu. Cahill once attended one of Wu Guanzhong's exhibitions, and had taken a photo with him on the occasion (Fig. 4-3). Later, in his paper "Styles and Methods in the Painting of Wu Guanzhong", Cahill lauded Wu as a master artist who successfully "fuse[d] western and eastern art into some kind of unity" and in whose work "we can see something that began as a confrontation of two artistic systems changing gradually to become a reconciliation of contraries". In 1994, during a visit over Qingming to sweep the ancestral graves, Wu Guanzhong painted the nostalgic *My Hometown of Beiqu Village* (Fig. 4-4), in which he recreates his childhood memories.

Today, the descendants of the Wu family remain familiar faces on the national and international stages of arts and culture. Wu Zuguang's eldest son Wu Gang is a photographer, his second son Wu Huan is an acclaimed artist, calligrapher, and writer, and his daughter Wu Shuang is a coloratura soprano and dramatist. Also from the same generation are Wu Ying, international concert pianist and head of the piano department at the Central Conservatory of Music, and Wu Bin, well-known editor at SDX Joint Publishing Company — the list goes on...

For over five hundred years, from the Ming and Qing dynasties through to the present day, the Wu family have played an inexorable role in China's political, economic, and cultural spheres. In imperial times, the Wus were a major family of scholar-officials, art collectors, and garden builders. In modern times, their participation in the 1911 Revolution and the founding of the Palace Museum, and their artistic productivity, have made them a prominent family in the

近代时期，吴祖光、吴祖强的父亲吴瀛作为"紫禁城接受代表"，成为中国故宫博物院的创办人之一。"九一八"事变后故宫文物南迁，吴瀛担任首位押运官，为保护文物付出了大量心血。吴瀛之父吴琳曾担任张之洞的幕僚，主持重修武昌岳王庙，弘扬岳飞"精忠报国"的精神。吴琳之父吴佑孙则协助张之洞创办湖北武备学堂，督练新军，使其成为晚清最具实力的军队之一。

吴祖光一脉皆出自迁居常州的洗马桥吴氏。在宜兴的北渠故里，也诞生了一位世界级的艺术大师——画家和美术教育家吴冠中，他是北渠吴氏第十九世。高居翰曾参加吴冠中的画展并一起合影（Fig. 4-3）；他称赞吴冠中的作品是"东西方艺术的汇合"，展示了"两种艺术体系从正面交锋，而渐渐互相妥协以致融合"（《吴冠中的绘画风格与技法》）。1994年吴冠中创作了油画《老家北渠村》，重温他少年时期的故乡记忆（Fig. 4-4）。

如今吴氏后人依然活跃在国内外的文化艺术舞台上。吴祖光长子吴钢是摄影家，次子吴欢是著名书画家和作

Fig. 4-3
1989 年高居翰参加吴冠中画展合影，莎拉提供

Cahill with Wu Guanzhong at Wu's 1989 exhibition. Photo provided by Sarah Cahill

家，女儿吴霜是花腔女高音歌唱家和剧作家，同辈的吴迎是国际一流的钢琴家、中央音乐学院钢琴系主任，吴彬是三联书店知名编辑……

明清以来的五百多年间，吴氏家族与中国的政治、经济、文化始终保持着难解难分的联系。吴家在古代曾是科举、收藏和园林世家，近现代以来，又因参与辛亥革命、创办故宫博物院、从事艺术创作，成为文博、戏剧、电影、音乐和书画世家。既让我们感受到一个世家大族深厚的文化积淀，也让止园不仅存在于故纸旧图上，而且延伸到今天的现实中，继续书写新的传奇。

spheres of museology, theatre, film, music, art, and calligraphy. In the Wu family, we can see the cultural sophistication of an old and eminent family, a family which, through their link with Zhi Garden, gives it a life that extends beyond the fragile leaves of old paper and into the reality of present existence — an existence that continues to generate new and inspiring narratives.

Fig. 4-4
吴冠中《老家北渠村》，北
京保利 2018 年春拍
Wu Guanzhong's *My Hometown
of Beiqu Village*, Poly International
Auction (Spring, 2018)

Timeline of
Key Events

止园大事记

时间	事件
1562 年	吴亮出生
1591 年	吴亮中举，为乡魁
1601 年	吴亮中进士，为会魁，授中书舍人（从七品）
1608 年	吴亮任湖广道监察御史（正七品）
1609 年	吴亮任巡按大同宣府御史（正七品）
1610 年	吴亮弃官回乡，聘请周廷策建造止园
1622 年	吴亮起任南京礼部仪制司主事（正六品），升南京吏部验封司郎中（正五品），改北京光禄寺寺丞（从六品）
1624 年	吴亮转北京大理寺寺丞（正五品），升北京大理寺少卿（正四品），七月初三日卒
1627 年	吴亮次子吴柔思聘请张宏绘制《止园图》
20 世纪 50 年代	高居翰在美国麻省剑桥首次看到 20 开《止园图》
1978 年	高居翰与园林学家陈从周在纽约大都会美术馆交流《止园图》
1982 年	高居翰出版《气势撼人：十七世纪中国绘画中的自然与风格》《山外山：晚明绘画》，以大量篇幅讨论张宏和《止园图》
1996 年	洛杉矶郡立美术馆举办"张宏《止园图》展"
2004 年	陈从周《园综》出版，刊印 14 幅《止园图》
2010 年 春	建筑学家曹汛发现吴亮《止园集》，与高居翰建立联系
2012 年 8 月	高居翰、黄晓、刘珊珊出版《不朽的林泉：中国古代园林绘画》
2013 年	园林设计师沈子炎制作止园数字模型
2014 年 2 月	高居翰去世

1562	Birth of Wu Liang
1591	Wu Liang attains his *juren* degree, having placed first in the provincial examinations
1601	Wu Liang attains his *jinshi* degree, having placed first in the metropolitan (*huishi*) examinations, and is appointed as a clerk in the Central Secretariat (a sub-seventh rank official)
1608	Wu Liang is appointed Investigating Censor of the Huguang Region (a seventh rank official)
1609	Wu Liang is appointed Imperial Investigating Censor of the Datong and Xuanfu garrisons (a seventh rank official)
1610	Wu Liang leaves the public service and returns to his hometown, commissioning Zhou Tingce to build Zhi Garden
1622	Wu Liang is appointed as a Secretary of the Bureau of Ceremonies, Examinations, and Education, under the Ministry of Rites in Nanjing[12] (a sixth rank official), promoted to Director of the Bureau of Honours under the Ministry of Personnel in Nanjing (a fifth rank official), and transferred to the Court of Imperial Entertainments in Beijing, where he was appointed Assistant Minister (a sub-sixth rank official)
1624	Wu Liang is transferred to the Court of Judicature and Revision in Beijing, where he is initially appointed Assistant Justice (a fifth rank official), and later promoted

止园大事记

12. In 1403, Emperor Yongle moved the imperial court from Nanjing to Beijing, and Nanjing's status changed from the empire's capital to its "accessory capital". However, it still retained all the organs of a central government. This included the six ministries, whose officials held the same rank and notionally performed the same functions as those in the court at Beijing, albeit at a smaller scale – governing Nan Chih-li province rather than the entire empire. In practice, officials were generally appointed to the Nanjing ministries in lieu of retirement, as a means of conferring honor without responsibility, or as a means of sidelining them from the centers of power.

时间	事件
2015 年	中国园林博物馆聘请微雕艺术大师阚三喜制作止园模型
2017 年	止园模型展出，出版《消失的园林：明代常州止园》
2018 年 春	宜兴博物馆馆长邢娟参观止园模型，联系到吴氏家族后人吴欢
2018 年 9 月	吴欢一行到洛杉矶郡立美术馆参观《止园图》，到伯克利拜访高居翰家人
2018 年 12 月	中国园林博物馆与北京林业大学联合主办"高居翰与止园——中美园林文化交流国际研讨会"
2019 年 4 月	北京那里小世界博物馆展出作品"止园记"长卷
2019 年 6 月	刺绣艺术大师孙燕云完成 20 幅《止园图》和高居翰头像乱针绣创作
2019 年 7 月	中国国际文化交流中心、中国文物保护基金会主办"明朝'吴氏止园'历史文化展"
2019 年 9 月	常州市委主办"《止园归来》视觉艺术展"，展出围绕止园完成的乱针绣、烙铁画、孟河斧劈石等非遗创作
2019 年 10 月	"园林：中国人的理想家园——基于绘画的明代止园复原"参加罗马尼亚布加勒斯特建筑三年展

	to Deputy Chief Justice (a fourth rank official). Wu Liang dies on 16 August 1624.
1627	Wu Liang's second son Wu Rousi commissions Zhang Hong to paint the *Zhi Garden Album*
1950s	Cahill sees the twenty leaves of the *Zhi Garden Album* for the first time in a museum in Cambridge, Massachusetts
1978	Cahill meets Professor Chen Congzhou at the Metropolitan Museum, New York, and the two engage in academic discussions on the *Zhi Garden Album*
1982	Cahill's *The Compelling Image: Nature and Style in Seventeenth-Century Chinese Painting* and *The Distant Mountains: Chinese Painting of the Late Ming Dynasty* are published, in which he undertakes an extensive discussion of Zhang Hong and his *Zhi Garden Album*
1996	The LACMA presents the exhibition *Paintings of Zhi Garden by Zhang Hong: Revisiting a Seventeenth-Century Chinese Garden*
2004	Chen Congzhou's book *Yuan Zong*, containing reproductions of fourteen of the leaves from the *Zhi Garden Album*, is published
Spring 2010	Cao Xun discovers Wu Liang's *Zhi Yuan Ji* and establishes contact with Cahill
August 2012	Cahill, Huang Xiao and Liu Shanshan's jointly authored book, *Garden Paintings in Old China*, is published
2013	Garden designer Shen Ziyan creates a digital model of Zhi Garden
February 2014	Death of James Cahill
2015	The Museum of Chinese Gardens and Landscape Architecture commissions intangible cultural heritage successor and master sculptor Kan Sanxi to create a large-scale model of Zhi Garden
2017	Kan Sanxi's model of Zhi Garden is exhibited, and the book *A Garden of the Past: Zhi Garden in Ming Dynasty Changzhou* is published

Spring 2018 Xing Juan, director of the City Museum of Yixing, visits the Museum of Chinese Gardens and Landscape Architecture to see the model of Zhi Garden, and contacts Wu Liang's descendent Wu Huan

September 2018 Wu Huan and his entourage visit the LACMA to see the paintings from the *Zhi Garden Album* in the museum's collection, and go on to Berkeley to visit Cahill's family

December 2018 The Museum of Chinese Gardens and Landscape Architecture and Beijing Forestry University co-host *James Cahill and Zhi Garden — an international symposium on Chinese gardens and Sino-American Cultural Exchange*

April 2019 Huang Xiao and Liu Shanshan's handscroll *Chronicle of Zhi Garden* is exhibited in Beijing's There Museum ("Nali Xiaoshijie")

June 2019 Intangible cultural heritage successor Sun Yanyun completes the disordered stitching embroidery recreations of the twenty paintings from the *Zhi Garden Album* and the disordered stitching embroidery portrait of James Cahill

July 2019 The China International Culture Exchange Center and the China Foundation for Cultural Heritage Conservation present the exhibition *An Unseen Page in Ming Dynasty History: the Wu Family's Zhi Garden*

September 2019 The Municipal Government of Changzhou presents the *Return of Zhi Garden* visual arts exhibition, displaying pieces centred around Zhi Garden created using intangible cultural heritage techniques such as disordered stitching embroidery, pyrography and Fupi stone bonsai

October 2019 *Garden: The Ideal Home for Chinese (Revival of Zhi Garden from the 17th Century Paintings)* is displayed as part of the Bucharest (East Centric Architecture) Triennale

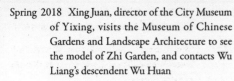

止园图册：
绘画中的桃花源

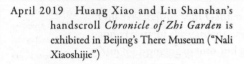

致

谢

2010 年我们开启止园的相关研究，恰逢止园建成 400 周年。感谢高居翰和曹汛两位前辈，带领我们进入这项课题。

这部画册能够出版，特别感谢美国洛杉矶郡立美术馆慷慨赠予 12 幅馆藏《止园图》图片的版权，感谢利特尔先生、孔纨女士、柯一诺女士的帮助。感谢吴欢先生为图册书写题名，刺绣大师孙燕云女士赠予乱针绣《止园图》版权，吴君贻先生提供吴氏家族文献，中国园林博物馆提供馆藏止园模型的照片，德国柏林亚洲艺术博物馆授予 8 幅馆藏《止园图》图片的版权。

研究过程中我们得到北京林业大学孟兆祯院士、李雄副校长、王向荣院长，中国园林博物馆张亚红馆长、刘耀忠书记、黄亦工副馆长，高居翰之女莎拉女士，美国普吉湾大学洪再新教授，加州大学长滩分校布朗教授，高居翰亚洲艺术研究中心余翠雁女士、白珠丽女士，高居翰纪录片导演斯基普先生、制片人齐哲瑞先生，波士顿美术馆亚洲部主任喻瑜女士，园林学家耿刘同先生、张济和先生，清华大学贾珺教授，北京大学方拥教授，中国美术学院张坚教授，北京故宫博物院周苏琴研究员，艺术家冰逸女士、安书研女士，常州大学葛金华副院长，联合国赴华项目负责人何勇先生，《洛杉矶邮报》任向东董事，常州学者薛焕炳先生、徐堪天先生的帮助，特此致谢。

还要感谢常州市委市政府、中国国际文化交流中心、中国文物保护基金会、美国加州大学伯克利分校艺术博物馆、中国紫檀博物馆、常州乱针绣博物馆、宜兴博物馆、北京那里小世界博物馆、北京文化产业商会、亚太交流与合作基金会、三联书店、活字文化、凤凰卫视、《常州日报》和《常州晚报》等机构和媒体的支持。

感谢出版策划秦蕾女士、设计师吕旻先生、编辑李争女士，使这部精美的图册得以呈现在读者面前。

Acknowledgements

Our research on Zhi Garden began in 2010, which just happened to coincide with the 400th anniversary of the garden's completion. Here, we would first like to thank James Cahill and Cao Xun for bringing us into and guiding us through this project.

The publication of this book was made possible through the generosity of many people. Special thanks go to the LACMA for generously granting free use of the copyright in the twelve paintings from the *Zhi Garden Album* in their collection, and to Stephen Little, Kong Wan, and Einor Cervone for all their assistance. We would also like to thank Wu Huan for providing the calligraphy for the album's title script, Sun Yunyan for granting copyright permission for the use of the pictures from the disordered stitching embroidery version of the *Zhi Garden Album*, Wu Junyi for providing the documents relating to the Wu family, the Museum of Chinese Gardens and Landscape Architecture for providing the photos of the model of Zhi Garden, and the Museum für Asiatische Kunst for granting copyright permission for the use of the eight paintings of the *Zhi Garden Album* in their collection.

In the course of our research, we received invaluable assistance from Beijing Forestry University Academician Meng Zhaozhen, Vice-Chancellor Li Xiong and Dean Wang Xiangrong; the Museum of Chinese Gardens and Landscape Architecture's Director Zhang Yahong, Secretary Liu Yaozhong and Deputy Director Huang Yigong; James Cahill's daughter Sarah Cahill; Professor Hong Zaixin of the University of Puget Sound; Professor Kendall Brown of California State University, Long Beach; Sally Yu and Julia White from the James Cahill Asian Art Study Center; Skip Sweeney and George Csicsery, director and producer of the documentary on James Cahill; Christina Yu Yu, Chair of Asian Art at Museum of Fine Arts, Boston; Chinese garden specialists Geng Liutong and Zhang Jihe; Professor Jia Jun of Tsinghua University; Professor Fang Yong of Peking University; Professor Zhang Jian of the China Academy of Art; Zhou Suqin from the Palace Museum; Artist Bing Yi, Ms. An Shuyan; Deputy Dean Ge Jinhua of Changzhou University; Ho Yong, Co-ordinator of the UN China Study Programme; Ren Xiangdong from the Los Angeles Post board of directors; and Changzhou scholars Xue Huanbing and Xu Kantian. We would like to take this opportunity to acknowledge their contribution and express our gratitude for their assistance.

We would also like to express our thanks to the Municipal Government and Party Committee of Changzhou, the China International Culture Exchange Center, the China Foundation for Cultural Heritage, the Berkeley Art Museum and Pacific Film Archive, the China Red Sandalwood Museum, the Disordered Stitching Embroidery Museum of Changzhou, the City Museum of Yixing, Beijing's There Museum, the Beijing Chamber of Commerce for Cultural Industries, the Asia Pacific Exchange and Co-operation Foundation, SDX Joint Publishing, Moveable Type Studios, Phoenix TV, *Changzhou Daily* and *Changzhou Evening News* for their assistance and support.

Last but by no means least, we would like to thank our publisher Qin Lei, designer Lyu Min and editor Li Zheng for their meticulous planning and thoughtful design that enabled this book to be presented before readers in its final, beautiful form.

参考文献
Notes and References

[1] CAHILL J．The Distant Mountains: Chinese Painting
     of the Late Ming Dynasty, 1570-1644[M]．New York &
     Tokyo：John Weatherhill Inc，1982．

[2] CAHILL J．The Compelling Image: Nature and Style in
     Seventeenth-Century Chinese Painting[M]．Cambridge,
     Mass.：Belknap Press of Harvard University Press，1982．

[3] 高居翰，黄晓，刘珊珊．不朽的林泉：中国古代园林
     绘画 [M]．北京：三联书店，2012．

[4] 黄晓，程炜，刘珊珊．消失的园林：明代常州止
     园 [M]．北京：中国建筑工业出版社，2017．

[5] 陈从周，蒋启霆．园综 [M]．上海：同济大学出版社，
     2004．

[6] 刘珊珊，黄晓．林泉不朽 名园重现——张宏《止园
     图册》与吴亮止园 [N]．光明日报，2018-07-01．

[7] 刘珊珊，黄晓．止园与园林画：高居翰最后的学术遗
     产 [N]．文汇学人，2019-02-22．

[8] 黄晓，朱云笛，戈祎迎，等．望行游居：明代周廷策
     与止园飞云峰 [J]．风景园林，2019（3）：8-13．

[9] 黄晓，戈祎迎，周宏俊．明代园林建筑布局的奇
     正平衡——以《园冶》与止园为例 [J]．新建筑，
     2020(1)：19-24．

[10] 黄晓，刘珊珊．17 世纪中国园林的造园意匠和艺术
     特征 [J]．装饰，2020（9）：31-39．

图册索引
Album Index

纸本水墨，画心尺寸：32.4×34.5 厘米
Ink and color in paper. Each leaf: 123/4×139/16in.

白底藏于柏林亚洲艺术博物馆
（Museum für Asiatische Kunst）
蓝底藏于洛杉矶郡立美术馆
（Los Angeles County Museum of Art）

图书在版编目（CIP）数据

止园图册：绘画中的桃花源 / 刘珊珊，黄晓著；中原
译. -- 上海：东华大学出版社，2022.1

ISBN 978-7-5669-1981-6

Ⅰ.①止… Ⅱ.①刘… ②黄… ③中… Ⅲ.①古典园
林 - 常州 - 明代 - 图集 Ⅳ.①K928.73-64

中国版本图书馆CIP数据核字（2021）第197794号

止 园 图 册

绘画中的桃花源

刘珊珊 黄 晓 著

中原 英译

策　　划　秦蕾 / 群岛 ARCHIPELAGO
联合策划　波莫什
特约编辑　李　争
责任编辑　赵春园
书籍设计　吕　旻 / 敬人设计工作室

出版发行　东华大学出版社
　　　　　（上海市延安西路 1882 号 邮政编码：200051）
出版社网址　http://dhupress.dhu.edu.cn
天猫旗舰店　http://dhdx.tmall.com
营销中心　021-62193056　62373056　62379558

印　　刷　天津联城印刷有限公司
开　　本　889×1194mm 1/16
印　　张　8.5
字　　数　286 千字
版　　次　2022 年 1 月第 1 版
印　　次　2022 年 1 月第 1 次
书　　号　ISBN 978-7-5669-1981-6
定　　价　258.00 元

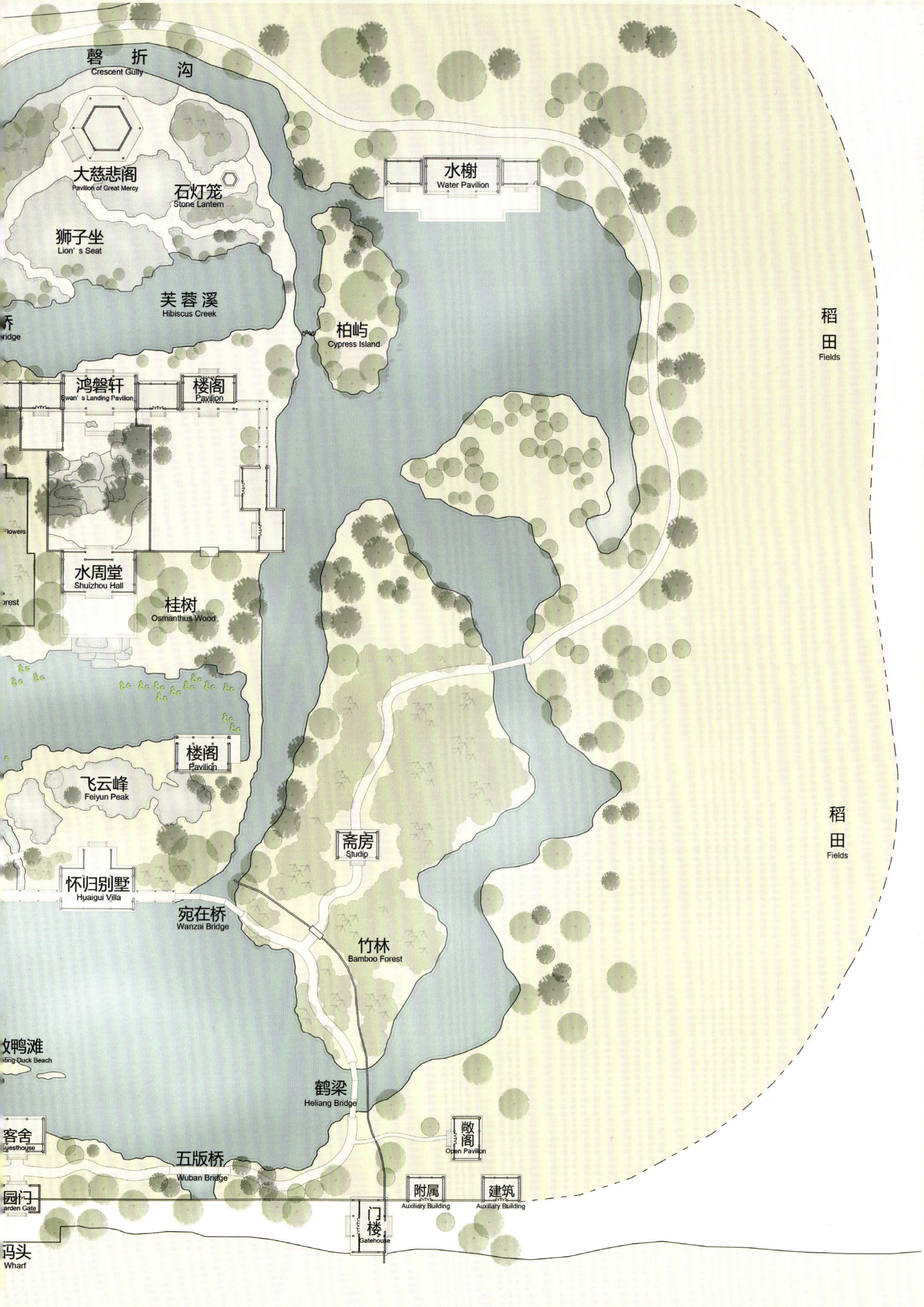

磐折沟
Crescent Gully

大慈悲阁
Pavilion of Great Mercy

石灯笼
Stone Lantern

狮子坐
Lion's Seat

芙蓉溪
Hibiscus Creek

柏屿
Cypress Island

水榭
Water Pavilion

鸿磐轩
Swan's Landing Pavilion

楼阁
Pavilion

水周堂
Shuizhou Hall

桂树
Osmanthus Wood

楼阁
Pavilion

飞云峰
Feiyun Peak

斋房
Studio

怀归别墅
Huaigui Villa

宛在桥
Wanzai Bridge

竹林
Bamboo Forest

戏鸭滩
~ing Duck Beach

鹤梁
Heliang Bridge

敞阁
Open Pavilion

客舍
~yhouse

五版桥
Wuban Bridge

附属
Auxiliary Building

建筑
Auxiliary Building

园门
~arden Gate

门楼
Gatehouse

码头
Wharf

稻田
Fields

稻田
Fields

The Zh
Z

止园平面复原图": 黄晓、王笑竹、戈祎迎绘
Reconstructed plan of Zhi Garden. By Huang Xiao,
Wang Xiaozhu, and Ge Yiying

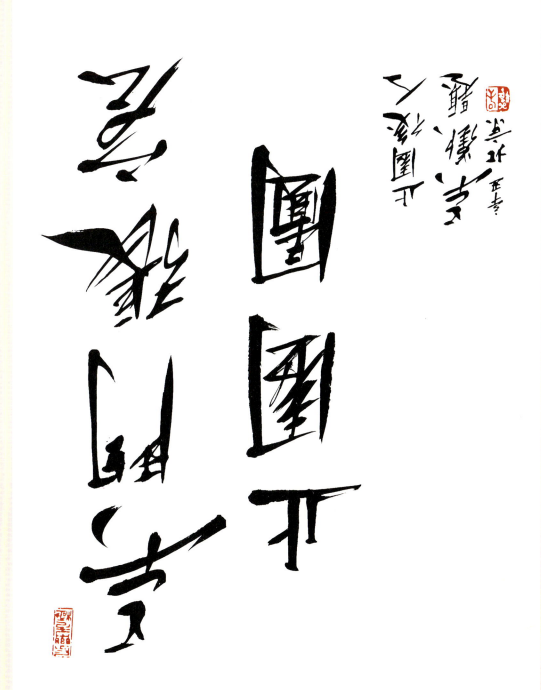

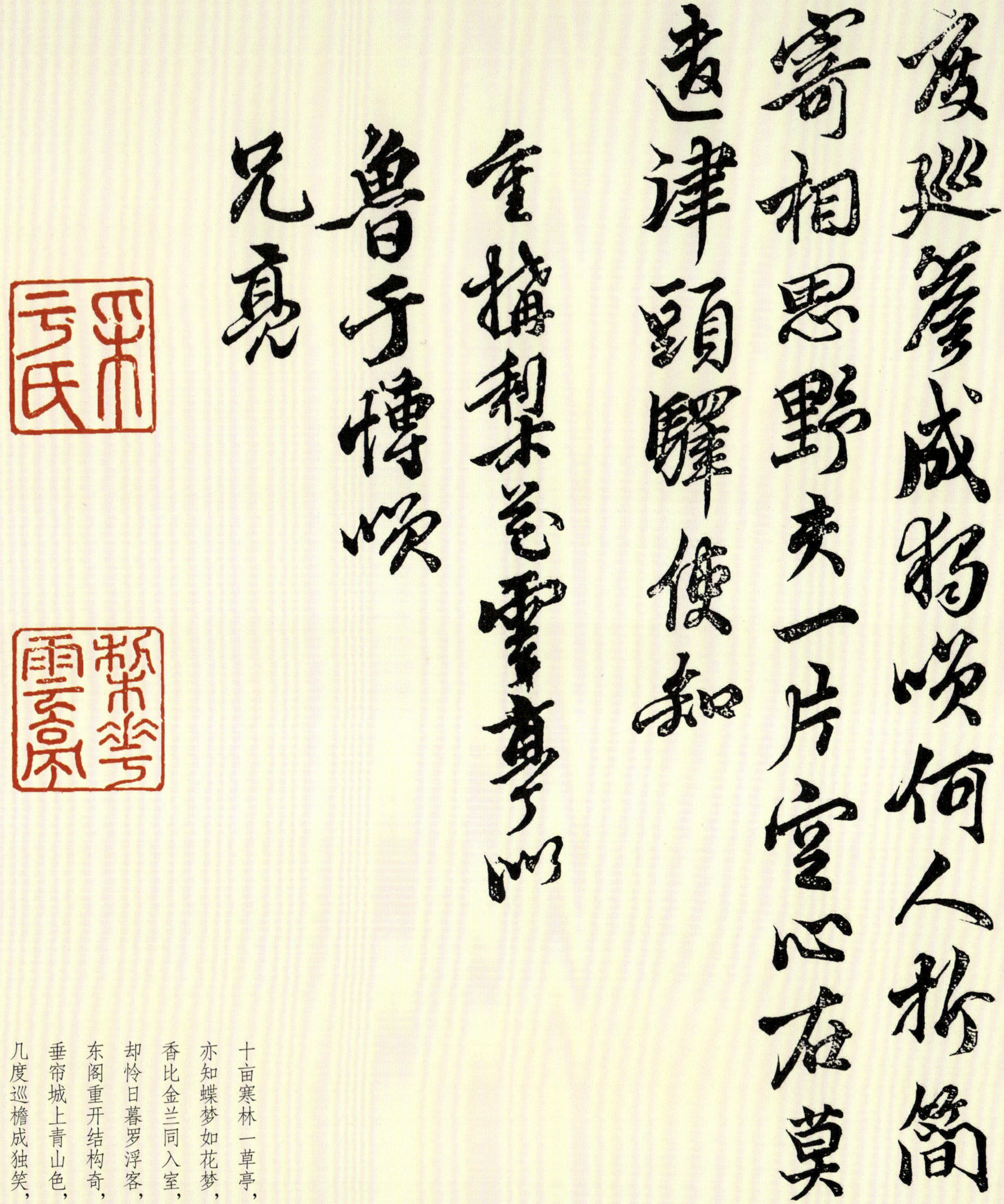

嗳延蓍成鹈顿何人扮简

寄相思野夹一片室心在莫

遠津頭驛使知

重搨梨苞雪亭州

魯于博頌

兄亮

十亩寒林一草亭，芙蓉为障竹为屏。

亦知蝶梦如花梦，安得身形似鹤形。

香比金兰同入室，光依玉树尽充庭

却怜日暮罗浮客，多少尘劳唤未醒。

东阁重开结构奇，欲从北渚问南枝。

垂帘城上青山色，对酒樽前白雪词。

几度巡檐成独笑，何人折简寄相思？

野夫一片空心在，莫遣津头驿使知。

重构梨花云亭似鲁干博笑。

兄亮。

印：采于氏、梨花云亭

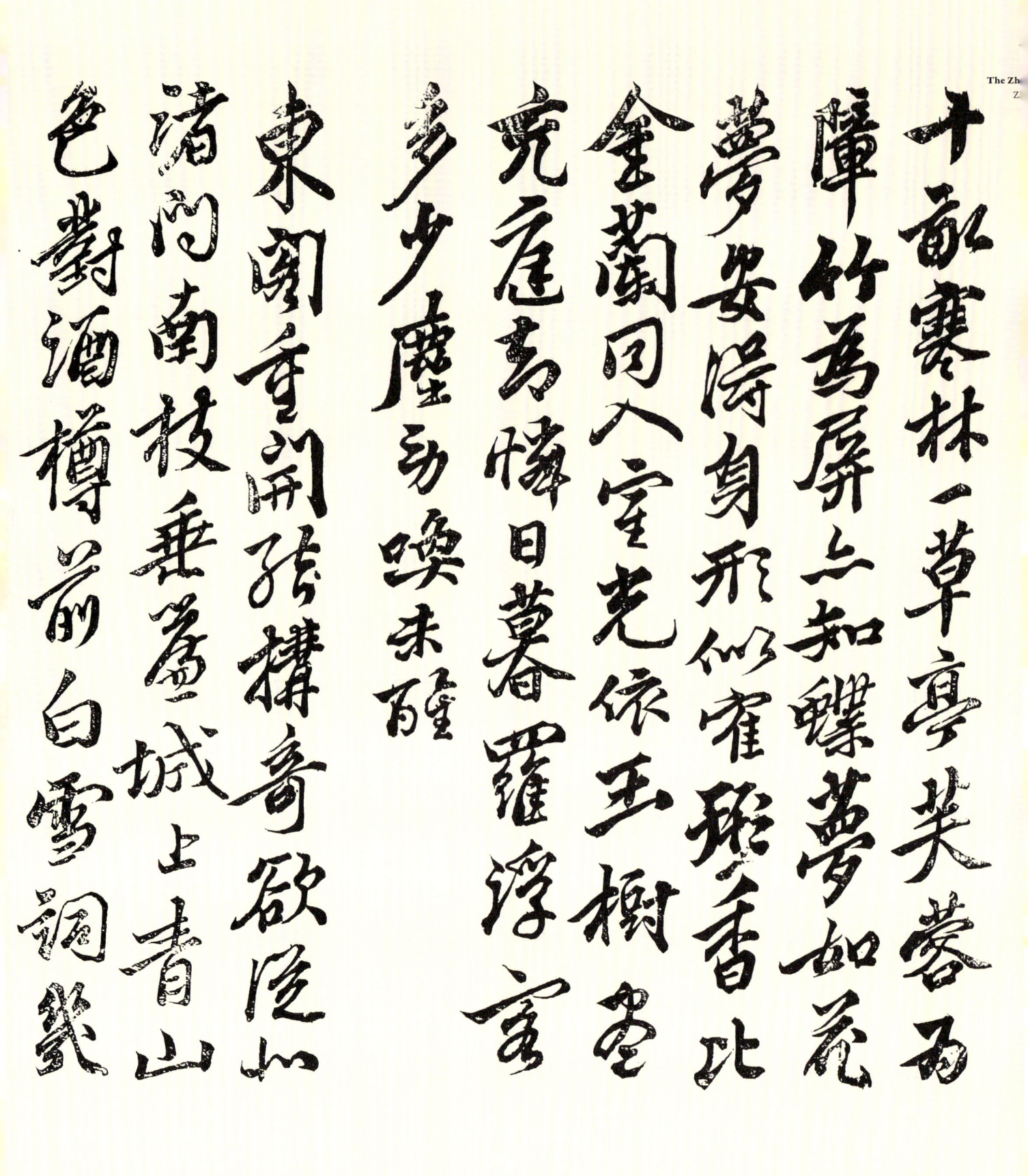

吴亮《重构梨花云亭》诗手迹。引自《家鸡集》
"Rebuilding the Pavilion of Pear Blossom Clouds"
Poem and calligraphy from *Jia Ji Ji*

天启丁卯夏月为徽止词宗写 吴门张宏

止园回望

竹香庵五首（集杜）

旁舍连高竹，风吹细细香。
兴来犹杖履，地僻懒衣裳。
易识浮生理，应耽野趣长。
谁能更拘束，白日到羲皇。

畎亩孤城外，村中好客稀。
自须开竹径，重肯叹柴扉。
筋力苏摧折，荣华有是非。
浮名寻已已，不厌北山薇。

去郭轩楹敞，无营地转幽。
众香深黯黯，野竹独修修。
茅屋还堪赋，桃源何处求。
欲浮江海去，从此具扁舟。

春来常早起，步屧过东篱。
放逐宁违性，幽偏得自怡。
美花多映竹，曲水细通池。
渐喜交游绝，闻樽独酌迟。

门径从榛塞，知予懒是真。
自多亲棣萼，幸各对松筠。
生意甘衰白，虚怀任屈伸。
修纤无限竹，处处待高人。

止园北门

清 止

萧斋自闲止，独对此君幽。
万籁声初寂，苍云满地流。

The Zh
Z

真止堂

真止堂二首（集陶）

行止千万端，哀荣无定在。
大象转四时，达人解其会。
误落尘网中，荏苒经十载。
山泽久见招，瞻望邈难逮。
怀此颇有年，闻君当先迈。
深谷久应芜，良辰讵可待。
谓人最灵智，鼎鼎百年内。
雷同共誉毁，诗书复何罪。
静念园林好，高莽眇无界。
茅茨已就治，紫芝谁复采。
从此一止去，今日复何悔。

仲蔚爱穷居，长公曾一仕。
趋舍邈异境，不学狂驰子。
少无适俗韵，我实幽居士。
暂与田园疏，久在樊笼里。
禀气寡所谐，志意多所耻。
心念山泽居，竟此岁月驶。
即日弃其官，行行至斯里。
欲留不得住，一往便当已。
聊为陇亩民，且当从黄绮。
寝迹衡门下，素心正如此。
吾生行归休，今朝真止矣。

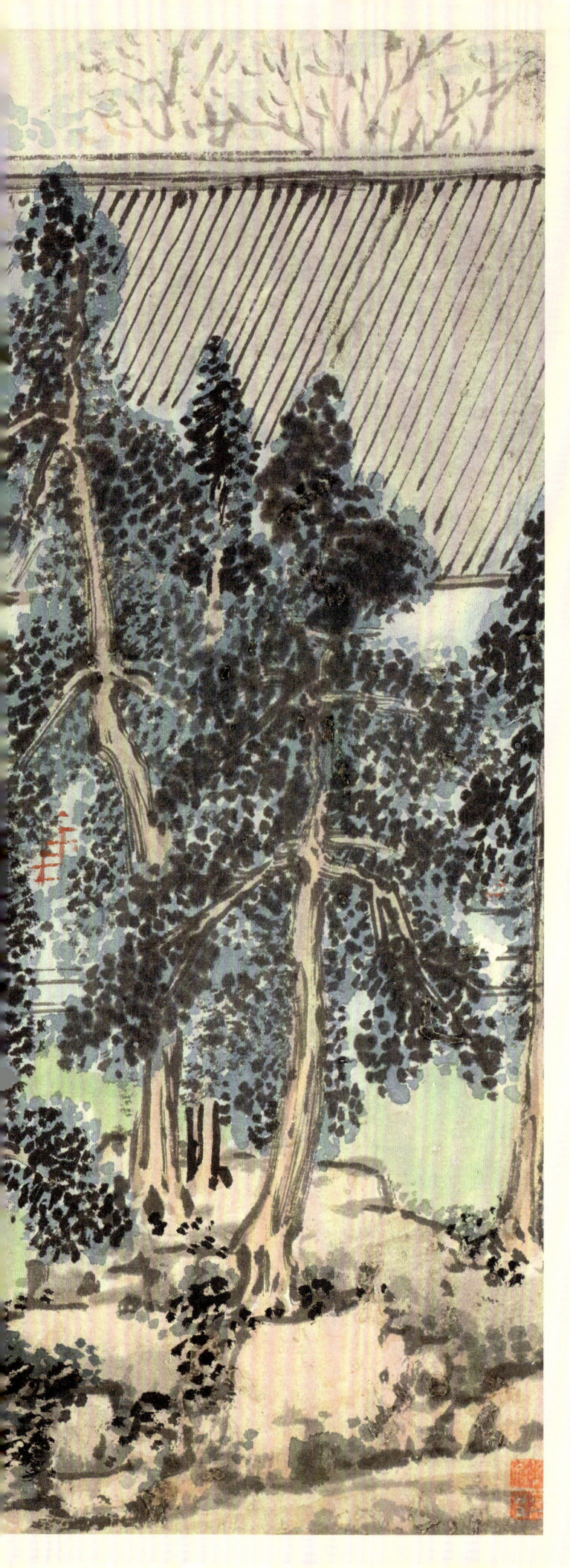

The Zh
z

坐
止
堂

坐　止

无事此静坐，一止止众止。
乃有坐驰者，山林亦朝市。

华滋馆与芍药栏

芍药栏

当阶红药烂春朝，露浥风翻茜未消。
士女若将相谑赠，牡丹应让一分娇。

The Zh
Zi

矩池西岸

北渚中坻（集骚）

帝子降兮北渚，执求美而释汝。
哀众芳之芜秽，独郁结其谁语。
世并举而好朋兮，又何芳之能祇。
折琼枝以继佩，纫幽兰以延伫。
搴芙蓉兮木末，贯薜荔之落蕊。
日康娱以淫游，恐年岁之不吾与。

矩池与桃坞

桃 坞

咫尺桃源可问津，墙头红树拥残春。

故园自有成蹊处，不学渔郎欲避秦。

规池与清浅廊

清浅廊

一泓清浅汇方塘，几树梅花护曲廊。

倚遍阑干明月上，半帘春雪散寒香。

印：张宏、君度

梨云楼

梨云楼

江南二月春光好，一气才新消息早。
罗浮山下雪乍晴，姑射峰头月方皎。
千树万树梅纵横，亚雪凌寒混月明。
片玉玲珑雕已遍，连珠点缀妆初成。
姑苏山水之窟穴，邓尉梅花更清绝。
香闻十里翠生烟，影落重湖白于雪。
忆乍移从江上来，繁英细叶枝头开。
城中一树不可得，此中琼岛疑蓬莱。
几度看花频载酒，登楼作赋重回首。
百岁无多雪满头，万事总看杯在手。
尽道迷花不事君，酒徒歌伴长为群。
林间酣睡香狼藉，梦中唤作梨花云。

The Zhi
Z

飞英栋与来青门

由文石径至飞英栋

振屧蹑崇冈，修筠碧于玦。
中有一径通，宛转乔虹蜕。
鳞甲忽参差，苍苔互明灭。
树杪呈穹阁，玄心蕴如结。
窈窕得平桥，银池界玉埒。
落英恋柔条，瓣瓣飞琼屑。

大慈悲阁

大慈悲阁偈

稽首大慈悲，具足诸法相。
虚空本刹那，光明无尽藏。
正观妙庄严，独见依昭旷。
我今发菩提，高阁自回响。
一室有皈依，十方无遮障。
尔时见世尊，从兹任天放。
不证亦不修，何得复何丧。
要知无住住，始会无上上。

Album

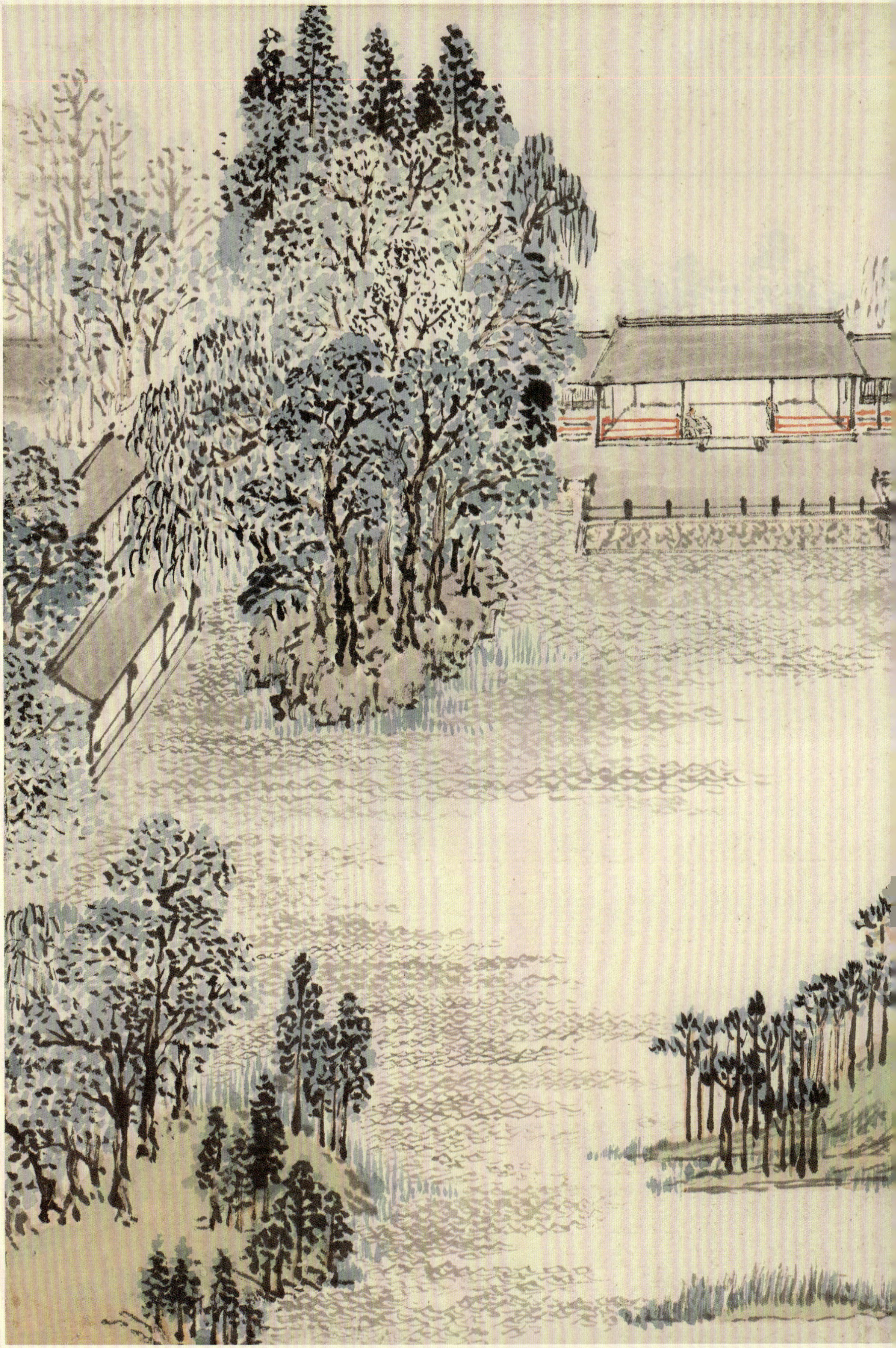

印：张宏、君度

The Zh
Z

柏屿水榭

由鸿磐历曲蹬度柏屿

礴砢谢崇丘，　轩楹瞰幽壑。

石磴故逶迤，　岩崖递岞崿。

列柏含青晖，　檀栾翠成幕。

凌寒更葱蒨，　迎风岂摇落。

上有双飞鸟，　衔鼓集林薄。

岂无台中栖，　弄雏自娱乐。

鸿磐轩

鸿　磐

鸿鹄摩苍天，徘徊视其翮。
浮云为低昂，须臾万里膈。
乌鸢自成行，俯啄仰相赫。
局促人间世，所志在于泽。
一举绝四海，不受罗与射。
临流理毛羽，安栖渐磐石。
陌彼枳棘群，逍遥矜所适。
指爪偶然留，冥飞亦无迹。

The Zh
Zh

水周堂

水周堂二首

负郭茅堂一水周，亦知吾道在沧洲。

避人只合亲鱼鸟，对客何妨应马牛。

满地江湖堪寄傲，连天滟滪不关愁。

倘逢渔夫遥相问，肯作湘累泽畔游。

层轩面面俯清溪，有客扶筇过水西。

深树云间知鸟倦，澄潭草浮识鱼肥。

烟波一艇青油幕，岁月双镶白板扉。

纵使菟裘生事薄，岂无片石选渔矶。

Waterfront View of the Peak of Flying Clouds

对望飞云峰

度石梁陟飞云峰

小山何盘陀，迤逦不盈步。
侧身度青霭，介然得微路。
疏峰抗高云，云阴莽回互。
徘徊抚孤松，恍惚生烟雾。
樛枝结菁葱，群葩借丹雘。
回展窅如迷，一步一回顾。

The Zh
Z

飞云峰

由别墅小轩

过石门历芍药径

开轩一何敞，在乎山水间。

侧径既盘纡，伏猊屹当关。

名花夹两城，吹动春风颜。

荒涂横蓁莸，呼童荷锄删。

点缀数小峰，文锦何斑斑。

径傍胜未尽，缓步还跻攀。

Album
g

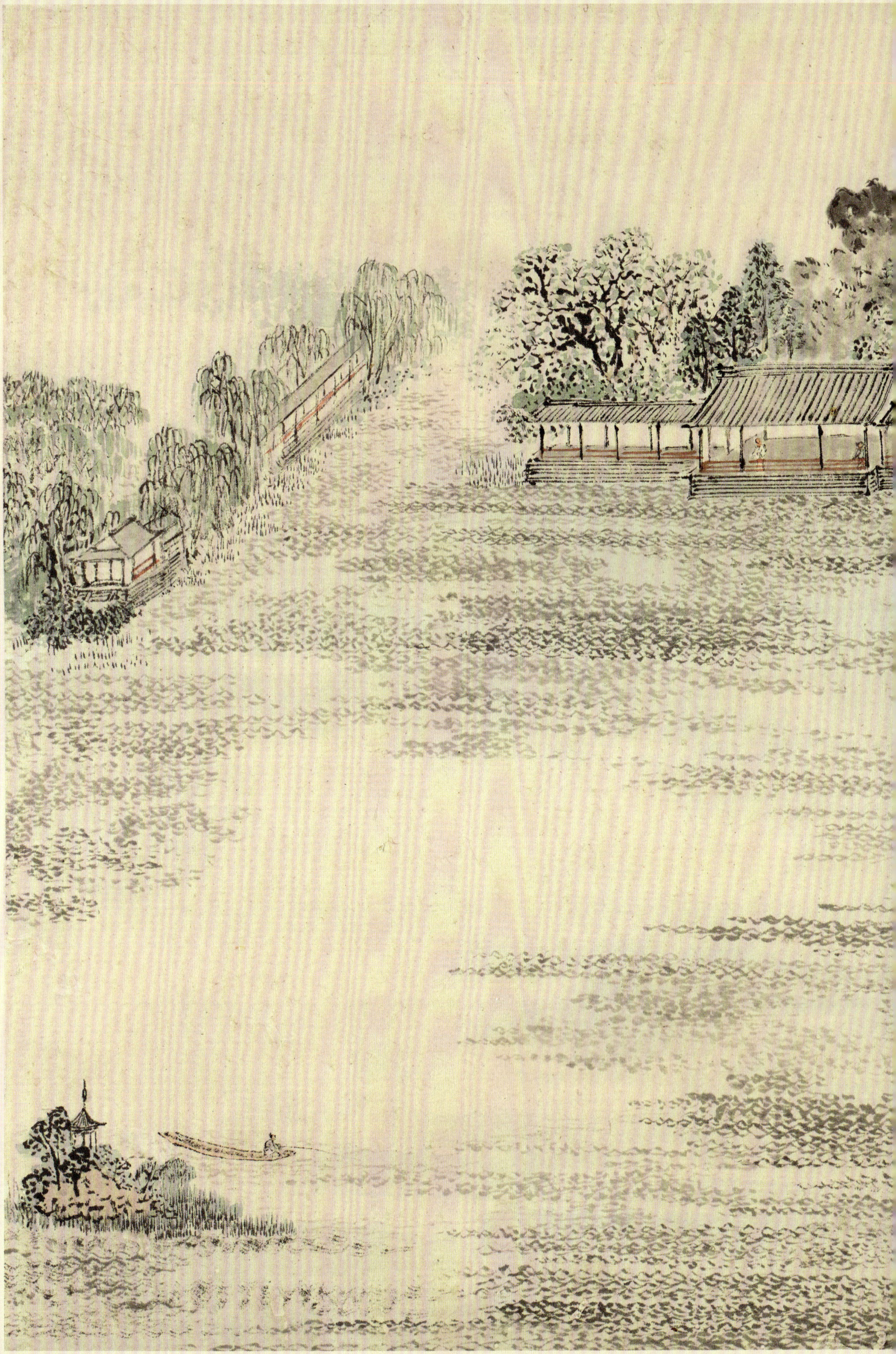

印：张宏、君度

怀归别墅

怀归别墅四首

吾道操竿拙，人情按剑深。
因歌出塞曲，翻动倚闾心。
岂谓波相及，应知陆渐沉。
一归万事毕，脱屣向山林。

日归归未得，将毋意何如。
世自工矛盾，吾宁畏简书。
千秋清议重，一夕主恩虚。
卜筑聊开径，怡然奉板舆。

封章先侧目，何处乞闲身。
歧路原无主，江湖更有人。
青山依北郭，流水过西邻。
此地堪高卧，飘然违世尘。

小筑犹迁次，移家就考槃。
只应逃市井，兼可废衣冠。
浊酒携樽尽，清溪倚杖看。
野人宁不愧，何苦恋微官。

The Zh
Zh

鹤梁与宛在桥

由鹤梁至曲径

万物各异等，贵贱安其常。
有鹤或在林，有莺乃在梁。
乘轩岂不荣，但忧天网张。
何如华池边，照影双翔翔。
奇音感哀咽，好貌多摧藏。
宁作阶下禽，三径犹徜徉。
竹实且不食，所谋非稻梁。

由曲径至宛在桥

委径隔疏竹，为桥有结构。
屈曲多余姿，林塘郁深秀。
盈盈漾轻绡，亭亭夏琼奏。
云阴度回溪，霞光媚清溜。
伊人宛在斯，道路阻且右。
溯回欲从之，褰裳不能就。
怅望秋水长，甘芳令人漱。

止園圖

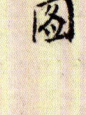

園門一帶

入園門至板橋

杖策入衡門，清風薄林木。
澄泓滎心神，雙渠匯寒玉。
忽作浩蕩觀，頓忘意局促。
杉條灑餘露，柳影依晴旭。
初徑誅新茅，崇梁依浚谷。
臨流一登眺，聊以送遠目。
望望蘆花洲，鳧鷺欣託宿。

止園全景
吴门张宏写
印：张宏 君度